GOD'S CHILD
IN THE CITY
CATCHING GOD'S VISION FOR URBAN MINISTRY

GOD'S CHILD IN THE CITY

CATCHING GOD'S VISION FOR URBAN MINISTRY

Billie Silvey

LEAFWOOD
PUBLISHERS

GOD'S CHILD IN THE CITY
Catching God's Vision for Urban Ministry
published by Leafwood Publishers

ISBN 0-9767790-0-5
Printed in the United States of America

Cover design by Rick Gibson

For information:
Leafwood Publishers
Siloam Springs, AR
1-877-634-6004 (toll free)

Visit our website: www.leafwoodpublishers.com

To Frank, Kathy and Robert—
who lived it all

Contents

Acknowledgements

With grateful appreciation to:

Michio Nagai, Calvin Bowers and Harold Shank, who helped shape my conception of urban ministry.

Mentors and teachers Jude Tiersma Watson and Lois Gomez.

The elders of the Culver Palms Church of Christ, who allowed me to serve.

Dedicated co-workers Ruth Johnson, Phil McCollum, Rona Kingsley, Sabeldi Jimenez and Merie Fregia.

Encouragers Gloria Crawford, Eloise Drake, and the late Jean Hager.

All the volunteers and students of the Culver Palms Life Skills Lab.

My long-suffering publisher Leonard Allen, and readers Frank Silvey and Diana Ryan.

Looking for Life in
All the Wrong Places

Do you ever feel as dead as Lazarus? Has the color, life and beauty of your faith leached away? Are you listening for the call of the Master to revive you? "Come forth!" he'll say, prompting your eyes to open on a bright new world, your shriveled limbs to move freely, and your heart to beat again with overflowing love.

The past few weeks, I've been reading Philip Yancey's book, *Disappointment with God*. I picked up the book in response to a major disappointment in my life. A ministry I had given myself to for the past eight years ended last year, despite my best efforts to save it. I was left shaken and filled with questions. Had I missed the point? Was this ministry not God's will? Hadn't he blessed it and led us through all sorts of difficulties? My first response was to feel depressed and profoundly disappointed.

I had been writing this book on urban ministry, and a couple of people asked if I didn't plan to drop the project since my ministry had failed. As soon as I heard the question, I knew the answer. I would finish the book. After all, I had been working on it since I first came to Los Angeles almost 40 years ago. It was an account of my experiences and the lessons I'd learned in those decades of living as God's child in this large city. My life, my experiences, and the lessons were no less valid because my ministry had ended. In fact, there was a chance that it would be more helpful to recount its failures as well as its successes.

After all, isn't that the way we live our lives—with mountains and valleys, straight sprints and long, slow detours? And when the failures come, are we really disappointed with God? Did he ever promise us unmitigated success? The incarnation and the crucifixion of Jesus answer that question with a resounding no. Jesus' life wasn't one continuous climb, and ours won't be either. There are disappointments in life, serious ones. We're disappointed with a doctor's report, a relationship, a job loss, a church dispute. But mostly, I think, we're disappointed with ourselves. We're disappointed with the powerless, colorless, unsatisfying nature of our faith.

When we read the scriptures, we know that disappointment isn't the ideal. We have God's Spirit living in us, and God's Spirit can do anything. "We know that in all things God works for the good of those who love him" (Romans 8:28). "We are more than conquerors through him who loved us" (Romans 8:37). "I pray also that the eyes of your heart might be enlightened in order that you may know the hope to which he has called you, the riches of his glorious inheritance in the saints, and his incomparably great power for us who believe" (Ephesians 1:19).

Why does our experience so often fall short of the ideal? Because we're looking for life in all the wrong places.

We look at the *World*. The world tells us that we're living in a post-Christian age, that Christianity is irrelevant, passé, insignificant to people today. I resent that. I know that my faith isn't irrelevant, but I also am terribly aware that it's not as relevant as it might be. It doesn't make the difference in my life, or in the lives of the people around me, that I know it could.

I see the New Testament apostles who "turned the world upside down," I see the Old Testament prophets, crying out against the injustices of their day, and I'm challenged to be more like them. Mostly, I'm challenged to be more like Christ, who "went about doing good." If I follow those examples, I—and my faith—will be anything but irrelevant.

We look at the *Church*. It seems to have answers, but they don't always satisfy, either. Reading church publications and listening to sermons, it often seems that, if we just managed to get it right inside the church building—to celebrate more in our worship, to assume the right posture when we pray, to discover the right way to approach Scripture, teach children, even do outreach—our spirits would be fed. We've tried it—endless varieties of it, and still we don't feel satisfied.

Maybe the problem isn't just what happens inside the church building. Maybe the problem arises from the other 90% of our lives, time spent at home and at work, at play and at study. Maybe we've tried to keep Christ confined to our church buildings when he wants to break out and change the world. "Let your light shine before men, that they may see your good deeds and praise your father in heaven," Jesus tells us (Matthew 5:16).

We look at *Ourselves*. If we could only get our inner lives and morality right, then maybe everything would fall into place. We'd feel a sense of accomplishment; we'd fill the emptiness; we'd be vibrant and happy. We want to feel good. We want to live close to God. But it doesn't always happen, does it? If we only turn inward, seeking our own spiritual fulfillment, we are bound not to find it.

That approach often is selfish. Maybe a better way to find good for ourselves is to seek it for others. "Each of you should look not only to your own interests, but also to the interests of others" (Philippians 2:4). I know that some of the most deeply satisfying, most truly joyful times of my life have been when I've given myself to help other people, when I've sacrificed my interests for theirs. "If anyone would come after me, he must deny himself and take up his cross daily and follow me," Jesus said (Luke 9:23).

Although there's a vital place for meditation, worship, education, fellowship, and searching the scriptures to find God's will, Churches of Christ have often emphasized these aspects of Christianity to the neglect of outreach and service to those in need around us, failing to meet them and help them where they are. That's part of our job, too. Political Conservatives say it's not the job of government to take care of the needy, which puts it squarely in our court. Liberals should be happy when needy people are helped, either by Christians or by the government.

And there's no better way to plug in members of the body than to put them to work helping others. We've tried getting involved at church. We've worn ourselves out with programs and projects designed to serve us and ours. But Christianity is more than increasing our personal holiness and strengthening our families. We need to reach beyond us and ours to touch a world in need.

Let's try getting seriously involved with our city. There's a payoff of life and joy for each of us as individuals. There's a payoff of vitality and growth for our churches. And there's a payoff of hope and fulfillment for the world around us. We'll be doing God's will, and we might just recapture the vitality, riches, and joy of believing.

This book incorporates autobiographical experience, scripture references, quotes from experts in urban ministry, practical suggestions, and the context of a real city to inspire and encourage each of us to minister to our own city, wherever that might be.

The first section contains four chapters on the city: the migration of people from rural to urban areas, the challenges of cultural and language barriers, the growing divide between haves and have-nots, and the fear of crime and violence.

The second section includes four chapters on the church: the problems faced by rural churches in an urban environment, building bridges to reach those in our communities, being like Jesus in the way we serve, and learning to trust God and his guidance.

The third section spends six chapters tracing the life of one specific urban ministry—the Culver Palms Life Skills Lab—from start up, to incorporation, to development, to its end.

The final two chapters summarize the book and return to the thesis of the introductory chapter—as God's children in the city, we find new life by serving others in his name, with his power, and trusting his guidance.

If we've been looking in all the wrong places for life and vitality, perhaps we need to look again, with God's eyes, at our own lives, our fellowship with other believers, and the mission he's called us to as his children in the city.

CHAPTER 1

The Call

In the summer of 1965, God called me to Los Angeles. Nobody saw it as a call at the time—least of all, me. Friends, relatives—even strangers—warned me away: "They're having riots out there. You'll get killed." "There's nothing but fruits and nuts in California. How will you ever fit in?" "People live wild in Los Angeles. You'll lose your faith."

I had grown up in the tiny West Texas town of Happy where the mournful wail of steam locomotives in the night set me dreaming of the large cities that were their destinations. During the day, we'd wait on the sloping grade of the railroad right-of-way as interminable freight trains crossed Main Street, their boxcars flashing exotic names— Chicago, Kansas City, Los Angeles—especially Los Angeles. I had been born in Sacramento when my father was in the military, and I was sure that the West Coast, the big city, Los Angeles was my destiny.

When I was 14, my family purchased our first TV set. Suddenly, the glamorous lives of city dwellers were right there in our living room. We could see streets lined with fine two-story houses and people wearing suits and dresses in the latest styles. The city promised jobs, education, opportunities. It spoke of wealth, sophistication and adventure.

Back then, not much was being said in Churches of Christ about God's call. Of course, I knew that God calls everyone to follow him, and I had responded to that general call in baptism when I was thirteen. As much as I understood at the time, I gave myself to him. But that God calls particular people to particular tasks was a notion that grew on me only gradually as I saw it work itself out in my life.

As Os Guinness writes in *The Call*, "The Caller sees and addresses us as individuals—as unique, exceptional, precious, significant and free to respond. He who calls us is personal as well as infinite and personal in himself, not just to us. So we who are called are addressed as individuals and invited into a relationship."[1]

God calls everyone to follow him and enter into relationship with him through that first, general call. He calls everyone a second way, but it is a more subtle, often progressive call. While some people seem to know instinctively what God wants them to do with their lives, others spend a lifetime working it out.

It wasn't until I came to Los Angeles that I began to hear that second, more particular call. Even though I wasn't aware of it at first—sometimes even fought against it—God was calling me to his work in Los Angeles. He called me gradually as I came to know and love the city and her many and varied people. I had come seeking the glamour and excitement of the city, but what I found was a heart increasingly touched by its needs—for the necessities of life, for knowledge, for purpose, for God.

Moving to Los Angeles marked the beginning of my forty-year interest in and commitment to urban ministry. In both paid and unpaid positions, I have served God by serving people in three distinct sections of the city. That, to me, is what urban ministry is—to serve God by serving the people in the community where you happen to live.

Urban ministry is varied. It includes ministry to youth, to the poor, to the addicted, to people troubled in body or mind. Anything we do to help urban people in need because of our commitment to Christ is urban ministry.

But why only urban people? Don't similar needs exist among all people? Certainly. While in the past Churches of Christ were a predominantly rural movement, spreading gradually into more urbanized centers in the South and Middle America, today more and more of us live in great cities—New York, Chicago, Los Angeles. Of course, one reason is a general shift in population. As rural populations dwindle and urban areas swell, more and more Christians find themselves living in cities.

But mostly, I believe this is happening because God is calling us to do a great work for him in these cities. God wants us to be where the people are—serving them and influencing them for him.

How can we keep from being overwhelmed by the size and pace of the city? How can we have an impact on the city rather than merely being impacted by it? How do we serve populations in need in the name of the Savior?

As a worker in various ministries in Los Angeles, I have often wished for guidance in how to do my job. As a trainer of workers, including annual spring break groups from Christian colleges, I've come to realize the need for a treatment of urban ministry that incorporates varied approaches and lessons learned. As a resident of a large metropolitan area, I've wished that more people had inspired me with a vision for the city. In other words, I've written the book I wish I had had, the book I so often felt I needed. My hope is that it will be helpful to other people as well. That it will inspire them, encourage them, and help them avoid some of the mistakes I've made over the years.

God's call may bring change

God may call some people to serve him right where they are, but his call to me meant tremendous change.

Nothing much ever changed in Happy, Texas. The skyline was punctuated by the same four grain elevators, the same businesses lined Main Street. I remember when they built the new post office, the bank, and the elementary school. That was about the only construction in the twelve years I lived there. I used to joke that the population was 642 when I lived in Happy—and 641 now that I'm gone. That stable childhood had become a bit boring as I reached my high school years.

Little about Happy prepared me for the changes I'd face when I came to Los Angeles. Even in 1965, Los Angeles was much larger than I had dreamed possible—and growing all the time. There were lanes and lanes of traffic in constant motion and sidewalks full of pedestrians. Airplanes shrieked overhead. Fire trucks and police cars whizzing past with their sirens blazing seemed to shake the sidewalk. Buildings were so tall, I could scarcely see the tops of them. How could there be so many people, and where could they all be going?

But coming to Los Angeles meant more than just changes in scenery.

It meant changes in relationships, leaving behind family and friends. It meant leaving all that had been familiar in a life lived, as long as I could remember, within a fifteen-mile radius. Within those fifteen miles were a loving extended family, a caring church, and a neighborly community.

Another change was a different approach to solving problems. In rural areas like the small town where I grew up, everyone went to church. The only question was *which* church. We all knew each other. If anyone had a need, everyone pitched in to help.

Large cities are more specialized. There's a clear distinction between my responsibility and someone else's. Partly it's because the problems seem intractable. Poverty, drugs, and violence are so pervasive there's really nothing I can do about them. Almost in self-defense, I confine myself to the smaller world of my family, my house, my job—what I feel I can manage. Doesn't the government have agencies to deal with the broader issues?

I knew everyone in my hometown and we spoke when we met on the street. The first few weeks I lived in Los Angeles, I continued the practice. But it didn't take me long to realize that, in the city, some men take a friendly greeting as an invitation to much more. I learned to stare straight ahead and ignore their remarks—just like a city woman.

Change is inevitable, but I personally resist it. I like to hang on to the comfortable, the routine. I'm not especially eager to be challenged. Yet, in an era in which technological advances make yesterday's methods outmoded before tomorrow dawns, where suicide pilots shake our confidence as readily as they do our buildings, I find in myself a surprising resilience. Could it be based on the stability of my early life?

There's another side to small-town life, though, and I had experienced that as well. It involves a lack of privacy and a pressure to conform that is inconceivable in the city. There were 642 people in Happy, and six different churches. In fact, as I recall, there was only one atheist in town—at least only one person who admitted to being an atheist.

Later, when I was a student at Abilene Christian College, the pressure to conform had become almost overwhelming. I knew girls in the dorm who would oversleep on a Sunday morning but then dress as if they'd been to church before they went to the cafeteria for lunch. They knew they'd better or they'd be lectured—not just by faculty and staff, but by fellow students.

That was one liberating aspect of transferring to Pepperdine College. Few people cared if you'd been to church or not. For the first time in my life, I knew that if I worshipped God, it was because I wanted to.

In moving to Los Angeles from a small West Texas town, my husband and I unwittingly became part of a river of humanity that is changing the world—the migration of vast populations from rural to urban areas. According to a study by Penn State, by the year 2005 half of the world's 6.5 billion people are expected to live in towns and cities, compared with less than a third in 1950 when I was eight.[2] That migration has continued, and even brought increased growth in the years since I've been in Los Angeles as southern blacks, Mexican peasants, and Vietnamese rice farmers have crowded into the city.

"Los Angeles County is America's most populous county," according to *Los Angeles Times* staff writers Maria LaGanga and Shawn Hubler in their report on the 2000 census. The addition of 656,174 residents in the 1990s brought us just short of our expected population of 10 million—two-thirds again what it was when we moved here in 1965. Almost 10 million people spread over a 4,000-square-mile area, creating a population density of 2,344 people per square mile.

Much of this growth has occurred in parts of Southern California that formerly were rural. "Los Angeles County's top three fastest-growing cities were all in the Antelope Valley, as the march of red-tiled, buff-colored homes pushed into more of Santa Clarita's canyons and the vast desert floor spanning Palmdale and Lancaster. Palmdale led the pack, adding 69.5%," the *Times* article continued.[3]

I've watched it happen, driving from Los Angeles to San Diego, to San Bernardino, to Santa Barbara, seeing housing developments, malls, and office buildings spread over what used to be barren hills and valleys. I've seen freeway intersections sprout where strawberries used to grow, watched new cities crowd out orange groves and buildings rise from what used to be a wild animal park. In the meantime, the central city has aged and deteriorated. "Los Angeles, in particular, is now an older urban area," according to William Fulton, president of the Solimar Research Group and senior research fellow at the Southern California Studies Center at USC.

Surrounding counties, such as Riverside and San Bernardino, which were sleepy rural areas in 1965, are becoming urbanized now, leading to traffic snarls and soaring housing costs over an increasingly vast expanse. Despite the small-town atmosphere some communities seek to maintain, "We are a far more urban area than we like to think," Fulton says.

In the past four decades, I've witnessed continued, even accelerating changes in the city itself. Los Angeles is constantly reinventing itself. Buildings are torn down and taller buildings rise in their places. The city has little sense of history. Only on the west edge of the city can we still see open space, and that's because we haven't yet figured out how to build on the ocean.

I wanted to live in an urban area. I wanted to leave the farm behind. But I didn't realize how much of it I'd brought with me—in my attitudes and approach to life and people. In some ways, I'm still that little girl from West Texas, gawking at the tall buildings.

Growing up in a small town gave me a sense of responsibility to those around me. Growing up in the church, I saw that responsibility as God's will for his people to help the needy and save the lost. I found it hard to ignore the plight of others or relegate the responsibility to social service or governmental agencies. I felt drawn to step in and do what I could to help.

God's call demands courage

Responding to God's call draws us out of our comfort zone. It brings risk and may make us afraid.

There was an atmosphere of fear—even paranoia—when Frank and I arrived in Los Angeles. The Watts riots had just ended, and the part of the city we moved into was still under curfew. The college was essentially a white enclave in the middle of a black area as large as several cities I had known. I had never seen so many black people before.

But despite my fears, I fell in love with Los Angeles at first sight. It seemed like a paradise in contrast with the dry, barren plains of West Texas. There were green, green grass, palm trees, and all kinds of birds and flowers. Everything seemed to grow larger here. To me, our part of the city seemed more like home than some other sections did. Most of the commercial buildings were two and three stories, set on mostly flat land. The houses were nice—one-story, single-family dwellings, mostly Spanish-style stucco with tile roofs, as large as the biggest houses in Happy. They were a little fancier than I was accustomed to, but not unfamiliar. Now they call the area where we lived South Los Angeles. At the time, we called it Vermont Knolls.

There were nice stores within walking distance. All the streets were paved, and they were cleaned every week. The sidewalks had curbs and traffic lights to cross with. And even though the streets turned out not to be paved with gold, the people were open and friendly. I became good enough friends with several black people that they didn't hesitate to point out insensitive things I said unintentionally and to explain cultural differences that puzzled me.

Not long after we arrived, we drove over to Watts to see the ghetto, anticipating New York-style tenements with people crowded onto fire escapes. The houses in the ghetto weren't so large nor the yards so well-kept as in our neighborhood. But that made it seem even more like West Texas to me.

A year after we moved to Los Angeles, my husband Frank joined the Navy and was sent to a ship off Vietnam. The war that had been little more than a series of news stories was suddenly a very real part of our lives. I wrote to him and worried about him every day.

Then one night in the spring of 1968, something happened that caused him to worry about me. My night class in English had just ended and I had stepped out into the second floor hallway when a student came dashing up the stairs. "Martin Luther King has just been assassinated," he gasped. "They're rioting in all the cities."

I stood stunned as everybody pushed past me down the stairs. When I finally got out of the building, the last cars were pulling away from the curb. I had a three-block walk to get home. It hadn't been three years since our part of the city exploded in race riots. What would happen after a tragedy like this? Despite the fact that I'd made friends among black people, I was painfully aware of my pasty white face as I started that long walk home. Was I safer clinging to the light of the streetlamps, or should I hug the shadows where I wouldn't be so obvious?

I finally got home, weak-kneed and trembling, but I'll never forget that metallic taste of fear in the back of my mouth. For the first time in my life, I was afraid to be seen in my own city.

God's call strengthens faith

God's call always brings change. It happened to Abraham in Genesis 12. God called Abraham to leave his country and family and go to a land God would show him. He didn't even have a road map. All he had was his faith in God and God's promises.

God's call meant changes for Abraham as it has for me. And as Naomi Rosenblatt wrote in *Wrestling with Angels*, "change requires courage."[4] In her chapter on Abraham, she quotes Anatole France: "All changes, even the most longed for, are melancholy. For what we leave behind us is a part of ourselves. We must die to one life before we can enter another."

It takes courage to answer God's call. We feel a tension between our desire for change and our fear of it. That's why God told Abraham not to be afraid "for I am your shield, your exceedingly great reward" (Genesis 15:1).

But even more than courage, answering God's call requires faith. Faith is the true opposite of fear. "Abraham believed God, and it was accounted to him for righteousness" (Romans 4:3). According to Rosenblatt, "Faith in the future is...constantly at war with fear of the future." People who believe in God have no reason to fear what the future holds. We know who holds the future.

The writer of Hebrews tells us that

> by faith Abraham obeyed when he was called to go out to the place which he would receive as an inheritance. And he went out, not knowing where he was going. By faith he dwelt in the land of promise as in a foreign country, dwelling in tents with Isaac and Jacob, the heirs with him of the same promise; for he waited for the city which has foundations, whose builder and maker is God....Therefore God is not ashamed to be called their God, for he has prepared a city for them (Heb.11:8-10, 16).

As we respond to God's call, we learn to rely on him

God has prepared a city for us, as well. It is a city we begin to experience as we answer his call, and experience more and more fully as we learn to see through his eyes and give ourselves to his control.

This is the promise that keeps us going—not the promise of "pie in the sky by and by," but the current promise of the blessings of a life lived in answer to God's call. It is this promise that guards us from despair, that helps us see the best in people and situations, that keeps us hoping and helping and working for the Lord—the promise that God sees what we cannot, that God can do what we dare not, that with God nothing is impossible.

We need to catch a vision of a city like Los Angeles as a city whose architect and builder is God. What would our city look like if more of its people heard and answered God's call? This, to me, is the real call of God's child in the city, to encourage people to hear and respond to God.

God's call requires commitment

Your call may be related to your interests and abilities or to your education and experience or to the circumstances of your life. Or it may have nothing to do with anything you've ever done or even thought about doing before. The primary requirement for hearing God's call seems to be a total commitment to doing his will. As Guinness puts it, "The key to answering the call is to be devoted to no one and to nothing above God himself."

Only when God is central to our lives can we give ourselves totally and eagerly to his work. As Guinness continues, "God calls us to himself so decisively that everything we are, everything we do, and everything we have is invested with a special devotion and dynamism lived out as a response to his summons and service."[5]

God's call can be progressive. God may call us to one ministry at one stage of our lives and another later. It's like Moses, who spent 40 years in Pharaoh's court, 40 years in the wilderness, and 40 years leading God's people.

My first ministry in Los Angeles was with the Lighthouse, an outreach ministry to neighborhood youth and children, sponsored by the Vermont Avenue Church of Christ and staffed by students from Pepperdine College. On Saturday mornings, we'd offer sports, tutoring, and games for the 30 to 40 kids who gathered there. That was when I discovered that I had a real gift for loving children and for teaching them to read using the *Good News Bible* and Dr. Seuss. We also wrote and performed dramas.

Later, when Frank and I had children of our own, God called me to a ministry of Christian journalism. It was work I had experience in, work I could do from home while nursing babies and supervising children at play. I got to know our neighbors and developed relationships that have continued through the years. They taught me the value of cross-cultural relationships and the strength of cultures not my own.

More recently, he's called me to work in involvement and outreach for a local church and in training people to get jobs through a faith-based nonprofit job training program. Even though they've differed, all my ministries have been satisfying and challenging. They've allowed me to know and impact the people of my city more directly than I could have without them. And they taught me more than ever to depend on God.

God's call brings blessings

Abraham traveled, and as he traveled, he worshipped God. I did the same. I had grown up in Churches of Christ, and I continued worshipping in Los Angeles with the Vermont Avenue church on the old Pepperdine campus.

Worship is recognizing God for who he is—holy and supreme, stronger and wiser and able to see infinitely more clearly and further than we can. When we realize that, accept that he is God and we aren't, and trust him to guide our lives far more wisely than we can ourselves, we can answer his call, wherever it takes us.

Because he obeyed God's call, God gave Abraham a homeland, made a nation from his descendants, blessed him and made him a blessing to others. When I came to Los Angeles, I, like Abraham, was blessed with a home. Los Angeles with its surging crowds and dizzying changes, its noise and traffic, is home to me now. I was blessed with a family. Our children grew up here and still live nearby. We get to see them most weekends. God has guided and protected and opened doors of service for me for almost four decades in different ministries in different parts of Los Angeles. I've been blessed, and I think I've blessed others. And my faith is stronger now than it has ever been.

Rosenblatt says of Abraham's blessing, "In simplest terms, a blessing is the unconditional love that a parent can confer on a child. It is a way for the parent to envelop the child with a sense of safety and care. We need the blessing of our parents' love in order to feel whole, protected, and connected. We need this feeling of being blessed in order to go forth into the world with a sense of purpose and responsibility."[6]

I had a good grounding of love from my earthly parents, but I was just beginning to sense my Heavenly Parent's love for me—the safety and care it gives, the wholeness, protectedness, and connectedness it brings—when we came to Los Angeles. I was just beginning to feel the stirrings of a sense of purpose, and a growing sense of responsibility for the people around me.

As I've grown in this sense of God's love and the security he provides, I've learned to trust him more. Not that I've overcome fear, but I've been able to reach out and bless others despite my fear.

God's call is a call to love

When I helped host college groups that came to Los Angeles for spring break, I didn't encourage them to consider urban ministry in general—ministry in New York or Mexico City, London or Singapore or Nairobi. I encouraged them to consider ministry in Los Angeles. We took them to Griffith Park Observatory as a part of their orientation, not to see the stars, but to look out over the spreading city and pray for its multitude of people. I had been called to Los Angeles, and I asked God to call others to work with us.

In an attempt to offset impressions of the city as evil, we taught those students about God's love for the city. We told them the story of Jonah. God called Jonah to preach to the people of one of the largest, most pagan cities of his time, the Assyrian capital of Nineveh. Surprisingly, those wicked urbanites repented at Jonah's preaching. Jonah was disappointed; he wanted God to destroy them. But God was pleased with their repentance and felt compassion for them. "Should I not pity Nineveh, that great city, in which there are more than one hundred and twenty thousand persons who cannot discern between their right hand and their left—and much livestock?" (Jonah 4:11).

God loved the people of the city, despite their lack of spiritual discernment. He wanted them to repent and turn to him, and he would show mercy. As Robert Linthicum writes in *City of God, City of Satan,*

> God feels sorrowful over the plight of the 120,000 adults and
> children of Nineveh as well as their animals, all of whom God

created. And God feels forgiveness for a wicked king and wicked people who don sackcloth and ashes and repent of the wicked things they have done. God loves Nineveh, just as God loves Jerusalem. God grieves over the city's sin and quickly offers it forgiveness.[7]

Jesus loves the city. We see it in his cry over Jerusalem (Luke 13:34-35, see also 19:41-44). As Linthicum explains this passage:

Here is God as the loving mother, seeking to gather her children to her and seeing them not only refuse her love, but scatter from her, rejecting her. Here are tears, here is compassion. There is only one word to express what Jesus is feeling here: hurt!—the deepest, most profound hurt. Such transparent hurt, such open-ly expressed hurt, such vulnerability, can only come from the most profound love. And for whom? 'Jerusalem, Jerusalem'—a city! God's city! Our City!

God loves Los Angeles, and as the song goes, "I love L.A." I love the freeways, the restlessness, the noise. I love the people, and the vast potential for good among those who will turn to God.

Maybe you feel that God is calling you to urban ministry. Pray about it, read about it, visit and study a city you might like to work in.

Maybe you already live in a city but aren't sure God has called you to ministry there. Look around for an established ministry and volunteer. It might be teaching literacy or helping feed the homeless. God seldom calls people who are sitting around waiting for him to make the first move. As you work, pray, asking God if another effort of that kind or of a totally different sort is needed in your city. What can you and your congregation do to meet that need? New ministries begin as Christians develop a passion for serving. If you feel unmotivated or uncertain, pray God to help you love your city with his love.

It doesn't matter that the city is large. It isn't larger than God's reach. It doesn't matter that we can't see clearly how to reach out to it. God sees and guides. It doesn't matter that the danger can be real and fright-ening. Faith overcomes fear, and God always wins. We may not see it at the time. It may look as if evil is triumphing on every hand. It has at times in my life. But God sees the way out, and if we continue to love and trust him, eventually we'll see it, too.

God's child in the city can be calm and confident, bold and venturesome, knowing who is in control. We can trust God as we answer his call.

Questions for Discussion

1. Why do people move to cities? Why do you live where you do?

2. What are some of the changes you've seen in your city in the time you've lived there?

3. Is God calling you to leave your comfort zone and serve people in your city?

4. Discuss the relationship between faith and fear.

5. How has God blessed you in your city?

CHAPTER 2

My Neighbor

Communication has always been important to me. I grew up helping my father put out his weekly newspaper in Happy, Texas. When I attended Abilene Christian College, and later at Pepperdine, I majored in journalism and English and wrote publicity for the schools. For 24 years, I worked as an editor with *20th Century Christian Magazine*. Since leaving the magazine, I've continued to write books, articles, speeches, and lessons.

Communication is important to me, but communication still is difficult. Even with those I know best—maybe especially with those I know best—communication is difficult. The Los Angeles Unified School District has identified 92 different languages spoken by children in the schools. Since there are many more racial, ethnic, and cultural divisions, communication can be strained indeed.

When I first came to Los Angeles in 1965, I worshipped with the Vermont Avenue Church of Christ. At that time, Vermont Avenue was a predominantly white church, serving mostly the students, faculty and staff of Pepperdine College. What is often the case—a certain tension between a college campus and the surrounding residential area—was exacerbated by the fact that the college was mostly white, while the surrounding neighborhood was black.

Over the next ten years, the church gradually became predominantly black as the college disengaged from the community—first by opening a second campus in Malibu, and eventually by closing the Los Angeles campus altogether.

It's called white flight, and it occurred in many parts of the city in the late 60s and early 70s, as blacks moved into formerly white areas and whites retreated to the suburbs. I'd hear white people—unfortunately, even Christians—whisper about "them." "'They' lower property values. 'They' are noisy. 'They' lead to increased crime rates." There were recriminations on both sides—many stemming from cultural differences and misunderstandings, others the result of overt racism.

Our God is the God of the whole world, not just people like us or people we're comfortable with. He made and loves everyone just as he made and loves us. He is a lavish, prodigal God who delights in variety. He made more kinds of insects than we can imagine, more kinds of birds and fish and animals. He made various kinds and colors and shapes of people, too. And he pronounced his crowning creation very good, because he made us in his image.

Sin has marred the beauty of God's human creation in general, just as it has each of us as individuals. That's why Jesus came—to save us from ourselves and "the sin that so easily besets us." His great love and sacrifice indicate the value he places on all human beings. "Red and yellow, black and white, they are precious in his sight." And they all should be precious in our sight as well, if we would be like him. Growing to have the mind of Christ means growing to share his nature, his values, his love, and his spirit of self-sacrifice.

As Jesus died for all people, we should live for all people—not in some abstract, feel-good way, but in practical acts that seek their benefit, even at a cost to us. Especially in a city of diversity, our unity can reflect the love of Jesus.

Racial tensions are a fact of life in urban centers, as immigrants pour in, not only from rural areas of this country but from both rural and urban areas of other nations of the world. Los Angeles is a vast crazy quilt of racial enclaves. As people "move up" from the old neighborhood to a new one with greater opportunities for employment or education, newer houses or lower crime rates, the borders between the quilt pieces shift and tensions result.

My neighbor may speak another language

The first major shift I saw after moving to Los Angeles occurred as Spanish-speakers from southeast Los Angeles moved west. I experienced the shift in a surprisingly personal and practical way.

The church I attended for 30 years is located on Vermont Avenue, a major north/south artery just west of the Harbor Freeway. It stretches over 20 miles from Los Feliz Boulevard in the Hollywood Hills to San Pedro on the waterfront. The church building is at 79th Street, almost midway.

I taught children's Bible classes at Vermont Avenue for 30 years, and most of the time I was there, we had an annual Vacation Bible School. We'd invite local families to send their children. My friend Elsie Tatum, who also taught Bible classes, and I would hand out flyers in the neighborhoods on either side of Vermont Avenue. At first, the entire area for miles around was native English speakers, mostly black.

Then, after several years, we began to find houses and apartments across the street from the building, on the east side of the avenue, where the residents spoke only Spanish. A Spanish-speaking congregation was meeting with us at the Vermont Avenue church, and as the number of Spanish-speaking households increased, Elsie and I began splitting up and going with a Spanish-speaking person to the east side of Vermont.

Eventually, it became useless for us even to cross the avenue, so people from the Spanish congregation worked the area east of Vermont while we confined our efforts to the English-speaking households on the west. By this point our entire VBS was bilingual.

Before I left the Vermont Avenue church in 1995, Spanish-speaking people were accompanying us house-to-house even on the west side of Vermont. The line that had been far to the east of us when I came had passed right over us thirty years later, as South Los Angeles went from being predominantly black to mostly Spanish-speaking.

Unfortunately, I heard the old whispers again. "They" lowered property values, had too many kids, and brought increased crime rates. And this time the whisperers were some of the very black people who had been whispered *about* a couple of decades earlier.

Language barriers like those Elsie and I encountered while inviting children to VBS began with the Tower of Babel (Genesis 11:1-9). Built to express the pride of a homogeneous group of people who asserted themselves against God, the tower was never completed. God cursed the people by causing them to speak different languages, which result-ed in their alienation from one another and their moving out in all direc-tions to become the various nations and cultures of the world.

As Milton Jones wrote in *Christ—No More, No Less*:

> The judgment against Babel was basically twofold. First, their language was confused to such an extent that they no longer hear and understand each other anymore. . . .
> Second, the judgment against Babel resulted in the splintering and dispersing of the tower builders. While this was certainly a judgment in one sense, it also helped fulfill God's initial intent in creation—multiplying and filling the earth.[1]

The story of redemption is the story of reversing the curse, reversing the dispersion of people until we all come together again in Jesus. Isaiah prophesied this reversal in 2:2:

> Now it shall come to pass in the latter days
> That the mountain of the Lord's house
> Shall be established on the top of the mountains,
> And shall be exalted above the hills;
> And all nations shall flow into it.

Isaiah tells of a future when people of all nations and tongues would flow together again. We see its fulfillment on the day of Pentecost (Acts 2). People had come to Jerusalem from "every nation under heaven." God's Holy Spirit filled the apostles, enabling them to speak in lan-guages comprehensible to all the varied peoples gathered there. Peter addressed the diverse group, telling them about Jesus, who had been crucified, raised to life again, exalted to God's right hand, and made both Lord and Christ. The people heard him, each in his or her own lan-guage! Talk about simultaneous translation!

As a result of Peter's preaching, three thousand people of differing cultures and language groups became one again in Christ.

Jones continues:

Resolution of the fall of Babel came in two areas. First, the people who had been scattered are now brought back together to become a people of community. A new fellowship, a oneness is created in the new spiritual dimension of the church.

Second, the Holy Spirit, who is poured out at Pentecost, opens the ears so that all can hear. Babel resulted in confusion of speech where no one could understand. Pentecost resulted in the miracle of everyone being able to hear in their own language. Unity is not achieved by human efforts but by the power of the Holy Spirit....

Even though acceptance of diversity is a popular plea, reconciliation by the Spirit is the only hope for bringing us back from the lostness of our dispersion to a unified culture of love.[2]

My neighbor may come from another culture

Working in urban ministry often means working cross-culturally, even with people who speak the same language. We came to Los Angeles just after the Watts Riots in 1965, and we were still here when burning and looting erupted after the Rodney King verdict in 1992.

The King incident came as no surprise to me. Watching the tape of the beating, I was reminded of the Mexican boy in my Wednesday night Bible class who had come to church a few months earlier with a gash in his forehead where a policeman had shoved him into a concrete bus bench. He was a quiet, well-mannered boy, and I couldn't believe he'd done anything to warrant such violence. The motto of the Los Angeles Police Department may be "To Protect and Serve," but most of my minority students knew that that meant to serve white people—and protect them against minorities!

Black and Latino teens, young adults, even mature men were routinely stopped by the police with little or no justification. Preachers for black churches habitually put on a suit and tie before driving through certain parts of town. My son, a tall blond, was never stopped when driving his car in our neighborhood, but his Latino friend was stopped both times he drove it without my son in the car. On election night in 2002, our new black State Senator was stopped by police on his way to his victory celebration! A few incidents like that may finally bring real reform.

Racial differences, especially language barriers, provoke all kinds of emotional responses—most of which are not Christian.

There's fear. We all tend to fear what we don't understand.

There's ego. If a person doesn't do things the way I do them, it's easy to assume that the way he or she does them is wrong. We know why we're doing something a certain way, or at least we think we do. When we see someone do it a different way, we may decide that their way is inferior—perhaps even morally so.

There's frustration. When we're trying to make a point, and the other person doesn't understand, we get impatient. The misunderstanding may be due to cultural differences or a language barrier, but the result is the same. We feel frustrated. We may even question the person's intellect. We've explained, even raised our voice to be better understood, and still they don't get it.

This becomes clear when we consider the differences among cultural groups in the perception of time. As Americans, we tend to be very time-oriented. We live by clock and watch, schedule and appointment book. The Japanese, often, are even more time conscious than we are. A friend of mine wrote a book warning Japanese business people of cultural differences that could lead to embarrassment. It included a delightful cartoon showing a Japanese person arriving at a couple's home for dinner to be greeted by the embarrassed couple still in their bathrobes!3

It happened in reverse when I was invited to a bridal shower honoring our Spanish minister's son and his bride-to-be. The minister was from Guatemala and his wife, from El Salvador. The bride's parents didn't live in Los Angeles, so I knew the minister's wife would be doing all the cooking for an event that promised to be massive. I decided to arrive early to help with last-minute preparations. Arriving fifteen minutes before the shower was scheduled to begin, I found her in her housedress, preparing food.

I panicked. "You run get dressed, and let me take over the cooking," I offered.

She looked at me as if I were crazy. "There's plenty of time," she said. "Nobody will be here for half an hour at least—probably longer." I thought she was a little strange, but as it turned out, she was right. She finished the food, turned off the stove, and went next door to their apartment to change. Though I stayed to admit anyone who came, she had changed and done her makeup and was back before anyone else arrived. It was my turn to be embarrassed. I had been ridiculously early for an event in their culture.

Cultural differences produce tensions

Another incident occurred when I worked with the Vermont Avenue church that illustrates the problem of cultural misunderstanding. We were planning a weekend event for youth. Everything was going smoothly until the question of food arose. The flyers we'd sent to other churches indicated that we'd be serving a meal. The white women of the congregation suggested hot dogs. The black women suggested turkey and dressing.

"Teenagers like hot dogs better," the white women said. "And they're easier to prepare."

"But we promised them a meal," the black women countered.

Back and forth the discussion went until it became quite heated.

Finally realizing that more was going on than just the question of · what food to serve, I talked with each group separately. It seemed that expectations, definitions, pride, and cultural differences all entered in. The white Christians seriously believed that teenagers preferred hot dogs and that hot dogs were an adequate meal. The black Christians were outraged. It would be dishonest to promise a meal, and then serve a snack. To them a meal meant meat and vegetables and dessert— something of substance.

Once we saw just where the misunderstanding had occurred, we were able to craft a compromise. Some of the black women offered to cook turkeys and the white women to bring desserts, and the event went off without a hitch.

As a result of misunderstandings like that, Calvin Bowers suggested that I audit his class at Pepperdine on "The History of the Black Church." He felt it would help me understand the source of the various cultural differences we experienced. Bowers was the Director of Ethnic Studies at Pepperdine and a minister for the Figueroa church, one of the oldest and largest predominantly black Churches of Christ in Los Angeles.

For an assignment in his class, I wrote a history of race relations in Churches of Christ in Los Angeles. Interviewing both black and white

pioneers, I discovered a history of sporadic attempts at fellowship with
breakdowns in understanding on both sides. As Lucile Todd writes in
her chapter in *Trusting Women*, "Experiences in the lives of black
brothers and sisters differ from those of white brothers and sisters, leading to different perceptions. Attitudes develop which, much like genet-
ic traits, pass from generation to generation."[4]

This variety of experience leads to tensions between people of different races, even Christians. And tensions, unaddressed, can lead to
division.

Two events that produced major schisms between black and white
churches in Los Angeles were the sale of the building of the old
Southwest Church of Christ to black Christians who had moved into the
area, and the sale of the campus of Pepperdine University to a wealthy
televangelist.

The sale of the Southwest building had to do with the considera-
tions that arise when a neighborhood changes. The Southwest Church
was a pioneer congregation among Churches of Christ in the city. Its
membership was white and remained that way as waves of black people moved into the area.

Bowers described the situation in his book, *Realizing the California
Dream: The Story of the Black Churches of Christ in Los Angeles*:

> On the local church scene, the Figueroa Church of Christ at
> 57th and Figueroa, was bursting at the seams, while only a few
> blocks away, at 64th and Normandie Avenue, the Southwest
> Church was literally dying on the vine....
>
> Then a strange thing happened. The Southwest church lead-
> ers began talking with A. L. Cassius and the leaders at the
> Compton Avenue congregation about the possibility of selling
> their building.[5]

Over the course of time, a church may totally change membership
as one person after another moves into the neighborhood and others
move out. In those circumstances, no one who was a part of the initial
congregation would consider selling the building to the group that eventually becomes the new congregation. But in this instance, the influx of
new people into the neighborhood wasn't matched by a corresponding

change in the makeup of the congregation. The shift from one group to another occurred abruptly and the two groups were of different races.

The original white Christians felt their members had invested in the property over the years and should get something back. The black Christians felt that a building intended as a meeting place for the church should be just that, whatever the race of the people now living in the community. Involved were subtle but unexamined cultural differences in views of money and property, race—even of the nature and purpose of the church itself.

The second blow to race relations occurred when the college itself moved out of South Los Angeles to a new campus in Malibu. Over the years, an increasing number of black students had enrolled in Pepperdine. The college was making an important contribution to a neighborhood where needs were increasing. But overall enrollment was dropping, particularly among students who could afford the high cost of tuition at a private college.

When news of the campus's imminent move was announced, churches in the area, most of which were totally black by this point, scrambled to gather funds to buy the campus to develop it as a school and social service center. The sale of the campus to a televangelist who had the cash in hand indicated to many that the college cared only about money and was turning its back on the city by not giving their black brothers time to raise the purchase price.

The animosity and hurt created by both events still affect race relations among Los Angeles churches today. They might have been avoided with deeper analysis, communication, and love. More listening, greater consideration as to how to treat each other as brothers and sisters in Christ, and greater faith in money matters could have improved relationships rather than intensifying the strain.

Cultural differences call for special efforts

Racial and cultural tensions plagued the first-century church as well. Despite their language differences, the original Christians in Jerusalem were culturally Jewish. Later, though, the church crossed a greater barrier than language by spreading from Jewish areas into Gentile ones.

The first incident of mixed Jewish/Gentile churches occurred in the city of Antioch.

Now those who had been scattered by the persecution in connection with Stephen traveled as far as Phoenicia, Cyprus and Antioch, telling the message only to Jews. Some of them, however, men from Cyprus and Cyrene, went to Antioch and began to speak to Greeks also, telling them the good news about the Lord Jesus. The Lord's hand was with them, and a great number of people believed and turned to the Lord (Acts 11:19-21).

Peter's preaching and his behavior in Antioch were inconsistent. "Before certain men came from James, he would eat with the Gentiles; but when they came, he withdrew and separated himself, fearing those who were of the circumcision." Because of this hypocrisy, Paul "withstood him to his face" (see Galatians 2:11-21).

Cultural barriers between Jews and Greeks in New Testament times were as great as the divide between Jews and Arabs today—or blacks and whites in 60s and 70s Los Angeles. But the Greek disciples in Antioch overcame the forces that would divide them from their Jewish fellows, contributing voluntarily to send relief to Jewish Christians suffering from famine (See Acts 11:27-30).

In addition to preaching to Gentiles on his missionary journeys, Paul made a point of encouraging contributions from the Gentile churches to relieve poor Christians in Jerusalem. Not only did this practice encourage sharing; it helped chip away at the wall dividing the two ethnic groups.

As relations between blacks and whites deteriorated, Calvin and I, together with Michio Nagai, minister of the Vermont Avenue church, and Evertt Huffard, who taught missions at Pepperdine, started the Ethnic Evangelism Seminars. We wanted to help local churches adjust to the influx of new ethnic groups moving into the city in a more positive way than whites had adjusted to blacks moving into formerly white sections of the city or blacks to Spanish-speaking people moving into formerly black neighborhoods.

Speakers in the seminars included Christians of various ethnicities sharing their experiences and faith, teenagers, including my daughter Kathy, talking about growing up in environments of racial diversity, and missionaries discussing cross-cultural adjustment from a scholarly perspective. Evertt presented studies on assimilation and the response of churches to changing neighborhoods. He and Calvin made me aware of what formal studies could contribute to an urban ministry. Before their teaching, what understanding I had was based solely on experience.

When our daughter started high school and began studying Spanish, I suggested that she worship on Sunday evenings with the Spanish-speaking congregation at Vermont Avenue. The Spanish preacher gave her a Bible and asked her questions in Spanish just as he did the other students in the Bible class. She was expected to respond in Spanish! It did wonders for her progress in her Spanish class.

It also did wonders for our family. Suddenly, we were a part of both English and Spanish congregations. We attended parties and weddings where everyone else spoke Spanish. During our fourth-Sunday combined services, I sang out in both Spanish and English, though I occasionally stumbled over the words. My husband Frank had lived three years in Rome and spoke excellent Italian, which was close enough to Spanish for him to get by. I managed with a lot of smiles and hugs and gestures, and we were able to help bridge the two congregations.

Another experience occurred after we moved to the South Bay area of Los Angeles. There, one of our neighbors was an Italian family. The parents spoke very little English. We became friends because Frank spoke Italian, even though I didn't. I spent so much time with these friends, though, that I came to know almost instinctively what they were saying.

Cira, the wife and mother of the family, got in the habit of asking me to go with her to conferences at the school as a translator. The teachers had trouble understanding her heavily-accented English liberally sprinkled with Italian words.

Finally, one teacher called me on it. "Do you speak Italian?" she asked.

I blushed. "No," I had to answer, "but I speak Cira." It was amazing how easily I understood things she'd say when the teachers and principal couldn't. Soon *they* began to ask me to come in and "translate" for her.

We see Isaiah's prophecy of language, cultural and ethnic groups coming together being fulfilled in Los Angeles today as people from all nations flow into our neighborhoods and churches. Or at least, that's the ideal—that all of us, despite race or culture, should be one in Christ.

It's been a continuing frustration as our family has sought to be a part of a neighborhood and a congregation that looks like we suppose heaven will look—diverse, with various colors and languages. True racial balance is elusive, in neighborhoods and in churches. It may exist tenuously for a time, but eventually it seems to teeter and drop off to one side or the other.

Now we live in the West Los Angeles/Culver City area, a richly diverse part of the city. The population is a mix of Latinos, blacks, whites, and Asians, as is my current church home and the people we served in the community outreach ministry I directed there.

Recently, I attended a Music Festival sponsored by the local Interfaith Alliance. Among the white choirs of the old-line Protestant churches and the tamborine-playing Hare Krishnas was the praise team from the Culver Palms Church of Christ. The members of the team were of various shades of black, white, and brown. They sang of love and brotherhood, and their very presence together communicated as loudly as their music did. It was the harmony of diversity that is becoming a reality where I worship today—a multiethnic, multilingual group of congregations meeting together in one building. On Sunday mornings, congregations meet in Spanish, English, Korean, and Chinese. The English-speaking congregation includes all the colors of the international rainbow.

We wonder how long the balance will hold in our new area, though we're encouraged by large communities from India, the Philippines, and Brazil in our immediate area and by the numerous Chinese students at nearby UCLA. They serve to balance the black population to the east and the Spanish-speaking area to the south. Even the white population seems to be holding between here and the ocean, supplemented by Eastern European immigrants to the northeast.

My neighbor may need my help

At the Culver Palms church, I took part in a ministry designed to help newcomers learn English, bring people together despite language barriers, and help people from other cultures learn what God has done for us through Jesus Christ.

It's called "Friends Speak," and it's part of the "Let's Start Talking" program, which has been used effectively for many years in evangelism on mission fields. "Friends Speak" uses the Gospel of Luke to teach English to non-English speakers in urban communities in this country. It's a ministry that can be used effectively in most urban areas to teach people from any country of the world. It's particularly well-suited for our neighborhood because, in addition to ethnic diversity, we have religious diversity with the Hare Krishna temple a block away and a mosque about a mile and a half from our building.

Not long after we moved to Culver City, I attended Urban Ministries Conferences in Dallas and Memphis. It was a culture shock to those of us from Los Angeles. These conferences, at least in the early days, presented urban ministry as white people from the suburbs going into the black inner city to teach and plant churches. That Southern model didn't fit our experience in Los Angeles, which involved people living in ethnically diverse neighborhoods, worshipping with ethnically diverse congregations, and ministering to people of various races who live in our own neighborhoods.

According to the *Los Angeles Times*, for the first time in history, Los Angeles County has no single racial majority. We are 45% Latino, 31% Anglo, 12% Asian and 10% African American. But despite the county's diversity, division remains. While broad areas may be mixed, neighborhoods tend to be predominantly one race or another. Even in churches where individuals of various races worship together, they may socialize separately. Only a few, mostly middle-class families, socialize across racial lines.

When I came to the Culver Palms church and began doing outreach in a multi-racial area, I enrolled in the mission department at Fuller Seminary, majoring in urban ministry and cross-cultural communication so I could be more culturally sensitive to the varied people in our community. We were just beginning our outreach ministry, and I took advantage of my Fuller classes to try out new ideas on educated and experienced urban church workers from all over the globe.

At Fuller I took courses like "Empowering the People of God," "Developing Leaders for Urban Ministry," "Biblical Economics and the Poor," "Church Growth/Effective Evangelism," a practicum in Urban Mission, and a directed study in Urban Mission, the latter two dealing with my local ministry. Our classes were taught by a combination of foreign and urban ministers, and each of them addressed the blessings and challenges of multiculturalism.

God can use my neighbor and me

Change is difficult, and churches and neighborhoods in ethnic transition are among the most difficult changes to adjust to. As Ray Bakke points out in his book *The Urban Christian,*

> The institutional church in a formerly stable parish is usually ill-equipped to face immigration, and its congregation seldom responds willingly or easily to the new realities. These churches may have had a foreign missions emphasis—"over there, somewhere." Host churches seem to have forgotten the virtue of hospitality. Christians need not trivialize or paternalize uprooted people by supposing that their immediate needs (food, shelter, employment or medical care) are their deepest needs; nor lump them into stereotypes; nor avoid personal involvement with them. Migrants may be driven into social isolation and be invisible though next door to us.[6]

Bakke calls us as Christians to catch God's vision, not just for foreign missions, but for ministry to those from other lands living in our own urban neighborhoods:

> In this increasingly interconnected planet where evangelism is now taking place on all continents, the churches at home must begin to model with integrity that which they have sent missionaries abroad to do. By sending them abroad in the first place, the church was confessing a transcultural commitment to the oneness of Jesus Christ. Urban pastors must practice it. Certainly there are skills required, but as in so many other areas, the key to handling urban diversity is not primarily a set of skills but a perspective on what God has been doing and continues to do in the world.[7]

Are you being called to minister across ethnic, racial, cultural or language lines? If you aren't sure, begin by respecting your neighbors of other races, cultures and nationalities.

Study another language, get acquainted with another culture. Read books by minority writers like Walter Mosley, Sandra Cisneros, or Amy

Tan. Even if you aren't being called to cross-cultural ministry, you'll be a broader, more enlightened citizen of your city and the world if you do.

Study the history of the ethnic groups in your area. Visit their houses of worship, whether or not they are Christian, and share your faith with them.

Make a conscious effort to befriend a person of another race. Don't just see her at church or at work, but invite her into your home. Acknowledge and confront racism in yourself and your church if you would effectively serve God and your multiethnic urban community.

Thanks to air travel, the internet, and email, our world is shrinking. We no longer have to cross oceans to be missionaries. The mission field is now next door or across the street. Be part of the future, not the past; catch God's vision as you encourage the flow of nations to closer proximity to one another at the foot of the cross of Christ.

As Bakke puts it,

> Few things are so spiritually satisfying as the personal discoveries
> of Christians that their faith transcends national identities or lan-
> guages and that the blood of Jesus Christ atones for sin across all
> human barriers such as geography, language, race or class.[8]

In a world in constant flux, where hatred explodes between racial and cultural groups, we need to remember God's vision of a mountain above the hills into which all nations flow like a mighty river of love and harmony. That is what the church is supposed to look like, though many have commented on the fact that, in most places, Sunday morning is the most segregated time of the week. God's child in the city needs to find creative ways to reach out in love and compassion to the varied and diverse people in the city. We must catch God's vision of unity in diversity and work to make it a reality in the cities where we serve.

Questions for Discussion

1. What are the major language groups in your city?

2. What is the ethnic makeup of various parts of your city?

3. What are the major difficulties faced by people from various cultures in your city?

4. How can you get to know more people from cultural backgrounds that are different from yours?

5. What steps can your church or Bible class or group of friends take to work with counterparts in another part of your city to help address needs?

CHAPTER 3

Extremes of Poverty & Wealth

As an assignment for a class at Fuller Seminary on "Biblical Economics and the Poor," my classmates and I found ourselves one afternoon in 1998 at the Biltmore Hotel in downtown Los Angeles. We were there to do a field investigation for a paper on the economic situation of people who live and work downtown.

The lobby of the Biltmore was warm and opulent. Vaulted ceilings with carved and gilded beams towered above marble floors, supported by massive marble columns. Brocade and velvet upholstery added sumptuousness. Exotic flowers filled the air with fragrance. Clear strains of classical music could be heard over the splash of a glazed tile fountain in the middle of the room, which gave the lobby the atmosphere of a Moorish castle. Upscale shops, including a florist and a boutique, were handy for guests, as were three adjoining restaurants.

A double staircase at the back of the room led to a registration desk upstairs. There we discovered that rooms at the Biltmore ranged from $225 to $2,000 a night. The Biltmore is a luxurious way to visit Los Angeles for people who live elsewhere.

After observing the hotel and its guests, we stepped back out into the brilliant sunshine and walked four short blocks east to the Frontier Hotel. The scene there was very different. Vagrants crowded the sidewalk. A large banner on the front of the building advertised rates of

$44.95 a week for a single, $54.95 with a full bath. Monthly rates started at $189—less than a single night at the Biltmore.

Shops and services at the Frontier included a store that advertised $3 clothes, a hair salon with yellowed posters of hairstyles, and a deli with no place to sit. A Snack Shop in the lobby consisted of a candy machine and a Coke machine covered with padlocked grates. Pinball machines and video games, a row of pay phones, a large sign advertising color TVs with HBO in the rooms, a display case with listings of the HBO offerings, and wooden benches separated by what looked like old-fashioned street lamps completed the decor.

At first glance, the Frontier seemed to have almost as much marble as the Biltmore, but on closer inspection, the walls turned out to be a thin, marble patterned composition and the floors, marble-patterned tiles. Everything was shabby and a little grimy. The Frontier is low-income housing, mostly for transients. Forty per cent of its occupants receive government subsidies.

Eight hundred people lived in the 424 units, including 62 children. A man from Louisiana who had resided at the Frontier since 1986 called it "a place to stay." The Frontier is an affordable place for people who don't have anywhere else to go.

When I told the resident manager that we were studying downtown hotels and had just come from the Biltmore, he laughed. "Four blocks and a world away," he said, pointing up the extremes of poverty and wealth that exist side-by-side in many parts of the city.

A professor painted the same picture of the downtown area, but in vertical terms. By day, executives arrive by helicopter at the tops of high-rise office buildings. English is the language of choice. Then at night, the scene shifts as cleaning people arrive on foot or in buses, speaking mostly Spanish.

According to a study by the YMCA, "The 90s have seen a greater polarization of income than at any point since the end of World War II. The middle class is no longer growing; instead, it is the top and bottom ends that are swelling. Since 1990 the wealthiest fifth of the population has seen its income grow by 21% while wages for the bottom 60% have stagnated or even dipped."[1]

According to the United Way, "Despite areas of great affluence, a persistent core of poverty remains with 15% of the population below the poverty line and 40% of households earning less than $20,000 a year."[2]

There's a persistent myth in America that we're a classless society. Despite our contention that "all men are created equal," and our lack of a formally recognized nobility, class distinctions are real and persistent. Even more than racial, divisions based on economics and education divide individuals, neighborhoods, even our churches. A middle-class person of any race can mix more comfortably with a middle-class person of another race than with a lower-class person of her own race.

These distinctions are based primarily on income, but they also involve education and sophistication—even style of dress and manners. The house you live in, the car you drive, even the food you eat can influence acceptance.

James denounced Christians in his time who showed respect for the rich while belittling the poor. "If you really fulfill the royal law according to the Scripture, 'You shall love your neighbor as yourself,' you do well, but if you show partiality, you commit sin, and are convicted by the law as transgressors" (James 2:8-9).

Why should it matter to us as Christians that some residents of our city are rich and some are poor? Didn't Jesus say that poor people would always be among us? (Matthew 26:11).

The results of poverty—ignorance, crime, blight, disease, and festering animosity over injustice—affect everyone. But it isn't just the results of poverty that should cause us to care. Robert C. Linthicum, in his book *Empowering the Poor*, points out that "the church is to be on the side of the poor, the oppressed, the exploited. It is to work for their empowerment—both by the gospel and by their own self-determination."[3]

In addition to teachings from both Old and New Testaments about serving the poor, Linthicum cites references to the practical effect of Christianity, including the example of Jesus himself. Jesus gives an example of how to feel about and treat the poor, both by his words and by his deeds.

Linthicum quotes from a third-century debate between the pagan Celsus and the Christian Origen:

In the course of the debate, Celsus reportedly declared,
"When most teachers go forth to teach, they cry, 'Come to me,
you who are clean and worthy,' and they are followed by the

highest caliber of people available. But your silly master cries, 'Come to me, you who are down and beaten by life,' and so he accumulates around himself the rag, tag, and bobtail of humanity."

Origen's response to Celsus' attack ranks as one of the most profound statements ever made about the power of Christianity. He replied,

"Yes, they are the rag, tag and bobtail of humanity. But Jesus does not leave them that way. Out of material you would have thrown away as useless, he fashions [people of strength], giving them back their self-respect, enabling them to stand on their feet and look God in the eye. They were cowed, cringing, broken things. But the Son has set them free."[4]

Poor people are everywhere. Why does poverty seem to be such a problem in the city?

The large population leads to concentrations of the poor in particular parts of the city. The wealthy don't want the poor in their neighborhoods, and the poor can't afford to live there anyway. Low-cost housing is voted out of well-to-do areas. It is demolished in urban renewal projects that fix up downtown areas to attract middle-class people while pricing out the poor, who lived there previously. The high cost of living squeezes many out of their homes and makes it hard to provide basic needs. Many people in the city are just one paycheck away from being homeless.

Advertising points up the contrast between rich and poor. It creates unrealistic expectations with messages like "You deserve…" and "Don't you wish you had?" It encourages immediate gratification, urging the poor, as well as everybody else, to spend rather than save any money they earn. It promotes unrealistic expectations like the lottery. And it promotes the use of nontraditional banking services, such as high-interest loans, check-cashing establishments, and paycheck advances that prey on the poor. Poor people are more likely to be victimized by these borrowing schemes because they distrust banks and often feel desperate for financial relief. Some frequent high-interest check-cashing establishments and then walk around with a month's pay in their pocket or purse, easy prey for pickpockets and purse-snatchers.

Jesus cared about the poor and oppressed. We are all too prone to care only about ourselves, our families, and the people we know. And all too often, the people we know are much like ourselves. It's not just a matter of showing partiality. It's a sign that we're selfish and indifferent. The challenge to us as Christians is to expand our area of concern, to reach beyond ourselves and share our goods, our abilities, our advantages, ourselves.

Our daughter Kathy grew up in South Los Angeles during the time when busing students from one neighborhood to schools in another was being touted as an effective way to integrate schools. One evening, I was talking with a neighbor, and I was feeling very indignant about the tone some of the busing controversy was taking: "You know I'm in favor of integrating the schools," I said, "but it does seem arrogant to assume that your children will automatically do better just because my daughter sits beside them in the classroom."

"Billie," my neighbor replied, "Don't you know that studies have proven that that's just what happens?"

I blushed deeply. Here was my black schoolteacher neighbor, the wife of an engineer, telling me that, just by our presence, we were helping people. I knew it was the case with immigrants who learn the language and culture better with increased associations with native-born people, but I hadn't realized that the same advantages could accrue to native-born people of other races or social levels. It was an eye-opening evening that left me feeling sad but more determined than ever to make a difference.

Extremes of Poverty and Wealth in the Old Testament

Los Angeles today is like Palestine in the time of Amos, the prophet. As Ronald J. Sider points out in *Rich Christians in an Age of Hunger*:

> The middle of the eighth century B.C. was a time of political success and economic prosperity unknown since the days of Solomon. But it was precisely at this moment that God sent his prophet Amos to announce the unwelcome news that the northern kingdom of Israel would be destroyed. Behind the facade of prosperity and fantastic economic growth, Amos saw the oppression of the poor. He saw the rich "trample the head

of the poor into the dust of the earth" (Amos 2:7). He saw that the lifestyle of the rich was built on oppression of the poor (6:1-7). He denounced the rich women (cows was his word!) "who oppress the poor, who crush the needy, who say to their husbands, 'Bring that we may drink!' (4:1). Even in the courts the poor had no redress because the rich bribed the judges (5:10-15).

Archaeologists have confirmed Amos's picture of shocking extremes of wealth and poverty....In the early days of settlement in Canaan, the land was distributed more or less equally among the families and tribes. Most Israelites enjoyed a similar standard of living. In fact, archaeologists have found that houses as late as the tenth century B.C. were all approximately the same size. But by Amos's day, two centuries later, everything had changed. Bigger, better houses were found in one area and poorer houses were huddled in another section."[5]

This picture drawn by the prophet Amos hardly causes us to bat an eye today. After all, don't we work so we can have a better standard of living than our parents did? Don't we want, not just to keep up with the Joneses, but to surpass them? What if others don't make as much as we do? Maybe they don't work as hard.

What is the Christian view of this phenomenon? Paul states it best: "For I do not mean that others should be eased and you burdened; but by an equality, that now at this time your abundance may supply their lack, that their abundance also may supply your lack—that there may be equality" (2 Corinthians 8:13-14).

That was the rationale for the equal distribution of food in the wilderness: "He who gathered much had nothing left over, and he who gathered little had no lack" (Exodus 16:18). It was also the principle behind the division of the land at the conquest of Canaan and the Jubilee laws whereby goods and property reverted to their original owners every fifty years. God is not glorified when we have much and others have little. God's desire is for equality.

The Extreme of Homelessness

We hadn't been in Los Angeles for a decade before we started noticing a phenomenon we hadn't been aware of before—suddenly, there were a lot more homeless people on the streets. There had always been winos and tramps, but they were mostly older white men who had made choices that, if they seemed poor, could be considered their own business. All at once, however, we were seeing many more homeless people of various races and nationalities, young and old, men and women. And there were children. Women were living on the street and in crowded shelters with their children.

There are many causes. People are drawn to Los Angeles who don't have the skills and resources to survive. Youthful runaways from across the country come, lured by the glamour of the entertainment industry. Homeless people are drawn by the moderate climate. You aren't likely to freeze to death in Los Angeles. But at a conference on poverty and homelessness sponsored by PATH, People Assisting the Homeless, I discovered that most of our homeless people are home grown.[6]

About the same time all these phenomena were converging, the State of California made a tragic decision. Under the guise of protecting human rights, but more likely because of budget constraints, they released people from mental hospitals. The theory was that the released mental patients would go home and be incorporated into their families and communities. However, some didn't have homes. Some had families who didn't want them or weren't able to care for them. Some were so maladjusted that they posed a threat to their communities and themselves—especially after they'd been on the street for a while and had stopped taking the prescriptions needed to treat their conditions. Jails and prisons began to fill in for treatment facilities in caring for the mentally ill.

Easy accessibility to stronger and more damaging illegal substances only exacerbated the problem, as addicts joined the mentally ill on the street. In fact, I still sometimes have trouble distinguishing between the two groups. Often they are the same people—whether suffering from mental illness brought about by drug use or abusing drugs in an attempt to cope with the demons caused by their illnesses.

One day our family was driving down the street when we came across a woman lying on her stomach in the gutter. She was inching her way out into traffic, wriggling like a worm. We stopped the car, and my husband Frank tried to persuade her to get out of the street. Before long, several people had gathered and were trying to help. Apparently, she thought she was in water and was trying to swim out. Unfortunately, "out" to her seemed to mean right into the middle of the busy street! Eventually, they were able to persuade her to get into our car, and we took her home. She promised all the way that she'd never take "angel dust" again, for the sake of her three young children she'd left at home by themselves.

Another day, a man came to church and walked right up to the front pew, scattering wadded-up bills all the way. One of the ushers followed him up the aisle, gathering the money and trying to return it to him. As the preacher began his sermon, the man threw more bills toward him. As he didn't seem to pose a threat, the usher just left him after finally succeeding in stuffing the money back into his pocket.

Another man disrupted the service, then walked out into the street, trying to stop the heavy flow of traffic with his outstretched arms. He thought he was invulnerable. People swerved and screeched to a halt, barely missing him until, finally, one of the church members talked him back onto the lawn. The disturbed man seemed to calm down, and the church member left to take him home. Later, we discovered that he had tried to jump out of the car as it sped down the freeway!

Ministering to Extreme Need

The Interfaith Council of the Los Angeles Coalition to End Hunger and Homelessness points out that

> Every day, thousands of Los Angeles County school children catch their bus at the shelter's door, hundreds of full-time workers use mats on the floor to get their night's rest, and many of our most vulnerable community members, suffering from chronic and often untreated mental illness, fend for themselves on the street.

The Council gave the following statistics for Los Angeles County:

- There are 50,000-85,000 homeless people on any given night.

- At least 10,000 are homeless children and youths.

- Nearly half the homeless adults work either full or part time and 76% were employed for some or all of the two years prior to becoming homeless.

- More than a third of homeless adults and youths are mentally disabled and almost half have one or more chronic health problems.

Joyce Young, a member of our Sunday morning Bible class at Vermont Avenue, felt called to do something to help the homeless. She suggested that we make sack lunches one Saturday a month, take them downtown where the greatest concentrations of homeless people were, and hand them out on the street. Six to ten women in the class made some 30 sack lunches each and piled them into a van. Then we car-pooled downtown, stopped on a promising-looking block, and began to hand them out. Suddenly, people came running toward us from all directions. We handed out sack lunches as fast as we could pull them from the van, and people still were running to get them after all the lunches were gone.

We did that for three years. It was a satisfying ministry in some ways. Most of the people were grateful, some asked for prayers, and a few wanted Bibles. But some would get angry if another person's sandwich was more desirable than theirs or if another person had gotten a drink or piece of fruit that they didn't. Tempers exploded until one day, two men went after each other, one with a pipe, the other wielding a board. Dwayne Lawrence, one of the men from Vermont Avenue, jumped in to separate them, and thankfully, was able to calm them down without being injured himself.

Gradually, the police went from helping us to trying to discourage us. There were health codes, after all. Most of the opposition, however, came from other church members. They felt it was useless to feed people if we didn't preach to them, or at least put a tract in the sacks. We tried that for a while, but it created an awful litter problem. "They won't know that you're Christians," church members complained. But time after time, people would ask us what church we were from or thank us with a "God bless." No one ever seemed to think we were members of some civic organization or atheist group.

Still it was frustrating. It was like putting a Band Aid on a bullet wound. At best, it was only a temporary fix, and at worst, it could do more harm than good. Homelessness is a symptom of broader problems, and gradually I became convinced that we were attacking the problem too late in the process. No matter what we did, there were more people who needed help, and the people we helped one day would all be hungry again the next. I longed for a more permanent solution.

The Working Poor

It isn't just homeless people who are poor.

In an article in the August, 2002, *Los Angeles Times*, staff writer Marla Dickerson pointed out that California children living in poverty are more likely than children in other parts of the country to live in a family with a working parent. "In contrast with the rest of the nation, where most poor children live in a household headed by a single parent, nearly half of California's poor kids live in a two-parent household."

She continues, referring to a study by the National Center for Children in Poverty,

> The Center found that most poor youngsters in California are the offspring of at least one immigrant parent, and that poor immigrant families are more likely to include a breadwinner than are U.S.-born families in poverty.
>
> Poverty experts said the study underscores the growing income inequality in California, where even unprecedented job and wealth creation in the late 1990s failed to close the state's poverty gap with the rest of the nation. With the economy now moving at a crawl and unemployment hitting a five-year high earlier this year, some worry that the chasm will widen.
>
> In 2000, the height of the state's economic boom, 18.6%, or 2.1 million, of California children were poor, compared with 15.8% nationwide.[7]

When I was working in community outreach for the Culver Palms Church of Christ, we borrowed an effective ministry to children in need from the Highland Church in Memphis, Tennessee. It was called School Store, and as we've adapted it here, church members donate backpacks and other school supplies, or the money to purchase them, on specified Sunday mornings near the start of the school year. The supplies are counted, and the money is used to purchase additional supplies needed to bring the total of filled backpacks to the number needed to supply the children expected.

Flyers are distributed in local public schools, and on the day set aside, the backpacks are handed out to students identified by their teachers, to needy members of our own English and Spanish-speaking congregations, and to others that our members know who might need them. It's been a wonderfully rewarding ministry that has given us a great reputation with the local schools.

Jesus, the Poor—and Us

A second community outreach ministry that enjoyed the support of schools, as well as social service and government agencies, was our free job training program. After the frustrations of handing out sandwiches on the street, I found the job training program tremendously satisfying. It allowed us to make a real difference in people's lives—to enable them to provide for themselves, not just give them things.

Speaking of the identifying characteristics of his ministry, Jesus said, "The Spirit of the Lord is upon me, because he has anointed me to preach the gospel to the poor; he has sent me to heal the brokenhearted, to proclaim liberty to the captives and recovery of sight to the blind, to set at liberty those who are oppressed; to proclaim the acceptable year of the Lord" (Luke 4:18-19).

Talking about the characteristics that should identify those of us who are his followers, Jesus said, "You are the light of the world....Let your light so shine before men, that they may see your good works and glorify your Father in heaven" (Matthew 5:14-16).

What can we as Christians do to help fight poverty in our cities?

1. We can help feed the homeless through a shelter or other homeless feeding project.

2. We can help train people to get jobs that pay salaries adequate to support their families.

3. We can encourage our congregations to get involved in feeding, housing, School Store and job training programs.

4. As our salaries increase, we can determine not to use the whole increase to improve our personal living standard, but to set some aside to help others close the gap.

5. We can ask God to use us and other Christians to reach out to our part of the city in his name, thus glorifying him.

According to Sider,

Scripture offers two crucial clues about the nature of economic justice that God demands. First, God wants all people to have the productive resources to be able to earn a decent living and be dignified members of their community. We should work to structure society so that all people who can work have access to the resources to earn a decent living in today's global economy. Second, God wants the rest of us to provide a generous share of the necessities of life to those who cannot work.[8]

Let's catch God's vision of equality, sacrifice and love. Let's make real his vision of his people as a city set on a hill drawing those around it like a beacon of warmth and love. As we reach out with Jesus' love and in his name to help the poor in our cities, we are being like Jesus and doing his work. And others will glorify him because of us.

Questions for Discussion

1. What are some of the economic problems in your city?

2. What are some ways people show distinctions based on income or education in your city? in your congregation?

3. What sorts of ministries could help the homeless?

4. What could be done to help people who have jobs but still are poor?

5. What changes could you make in your lifestyle to make more money available to help people?

CHAPTER 4

Crime and Violence

It was Wednesday night, and I had just finished teaching a Bible lesson to about ten of the "big kids" in our congregation. Attendance at midweek services at the Vermont Avenue church was low enough that we only had two children's classes—the big kids and the little kids. The big kids were the ones who could read.

I straightened the classroom for the teacher who'd be using it on Sunday morning, gathered my materials, and had just started down the stairs when I saw strange colored lights sweeping the window. As I opened the side door onto the alley that deadended at our building, I was confronted by a scene that froze my blood. Yellow police tape was stretched across the entrance to the alley, police officers with walkie-talkies milled around our dumpster, and police car radios squawked, their lights sweeping the side of the building.

"What happened?" I gasped.

"We found a body in the dumpster," one of the officers said in a matter-of-fact tone. It wasn't at all matter-of-fact to me. My mind raced. How many students had gone out that door ahead of me, and how many had turned through the kitchen and into the Fellowship Hall to meet their parents? Many of our students walked from neighboring houses, just as I did, and, just as I did, would have walked right out the door and into a murder scene.

Most of those neighborhood children came to Bible class on their own. Their parents weren't a part of our church. It was one of the delights of teaching classes in South Los Angeles that neighborhood children got excited about coming to Bible class, if only for something to do at night.

The next week, I scrapped my planned lesson to allow for a discussion of what had happened the week before. When I mentioned it to the students, one of them shrugged. "It happens all the time," she said.

She was right. We lived in the 77th precinct, the section of Los Angeles with the highest crime rate in the city. While homicides didn't take place "all the time," they were much too frequent. Often the victims were innocent. It wasn't so much random violence as poor marksmanship. Frightened, often "hopped up" gang members don't make the world's most accurate shooters.

We talked about family members—uncles and brothers and cousins—who had been killed. We talked about neighbors and friends. Few of the children had remained untouched.

We talked about our response to violence. Many wanted to take a gun and go after the guys who had killed their family members and friends. The concept of turning the other cheek elicited more snickers than serious consideration. "God can't really expect us to do that," was the incredulous response.

As we continued discussing violence, my heart was breaking over the shells the children had been forced to develop to protect themselves from pain. What they had seen and experienced had caused them to grow up—and grow harder—much faster than I hoped my own children would, than children in my previous experience had.

Several years later, I attended my first funeral for a gang member. The young man was the son of a fine couple from our Spanish congregation. He had been trying to get out of the gang for some time. In fact, the family had moved out of the area in an attempt to escape. But leaving a gang isn't that easy. The gang members found him, chased him home, and executed him on the back porch as he reached for the doorknob.

The funeral was held in a small chapel on the grounds of Forest Lawn Mortuary, far from our neighborhood. Michio Nagai, our minister, was halfway through the service when the gang members arrived. They filed in the back door, walked to the front and surrounded the casket. Michio asked them to sit down and join us and continued speaking. A slight, soft-spoken man, he was capable of exceptional strength. That was one of several times I saw him display it.

Responses to Violence

Eventually, we moved from South Los Angeles to the South Bay. It was close enough that I still worshipped with the Vermont Avenue church, but far enough out of the totally black neighborhood that our kids were able to attend racially diverse schools.

One night in 1992, I was walking out to the car with my box of materials for Wednesday night Bible class when my husband Frank came home from work.

"Are you planning to go in to teach tonight?" he asked.

"Of course, I've got the lesson all ready." Then I stopped. Something about his expression told me something was wrong. "Why not?"

"Have you had the TV on today?"

"No, I've been working all day." As an editor for *20th Century Christian* magazine, I worked out of my house.

"Well, I think you'd better come back in and turn it on. You might want to stay home tonight."

I turned around and went back into the house, shaking my head. What could make me stay home when the kids would be waiting for a Bible lesson? As the TV flickered on, I was shocked to see our city in flames again, and this time the scene was chillingly familiar. Vermont Avenue was burning. I saw the Dominos Pizza just down the street from the church building, where I called to have pizzas delivered for an occasional party after class, and the Swap Meet across the street from it. A large part of both sides of Vermont Avenue, less than a block from our church building, was burning to the ground!

We called our children, then watched transfixed as first one part of the city, and then another, burst into flames. The disturbance had begun on Normandie Avenue, only blocks from our home of ten years.

When our son Robert got off work, he came over with some friends. We sat in shock watching burning buildings, rioting crowds, and confused newscasters who obviously had never been in the parts of the city where the news was taking place.

The next day, I called to see if the church building was still standing and to check on a former neighbor. "I'm getting groceries today," I
told her, "Can I pick up some things for you?"

"You'd better just stay away," she said. "We even told our children
not to come."

When I got to the grocery store, it was packed with people who
were hoarding food, people who had driven miles just to find a store
that was open. We waited in lines that stretched to the back of the building, then had to bag our own groceries. As we waited, we talked and
joked with strangers. I'd never seen people in Los Angeles behaving so
courteously—"Excuse me," "I'm sorry," "Could I please?" The tension was
so thick it was palpable. We were afraid of each other. We were afraid
of what we ourselves might be capable of if things got out of hand.

The next Saturday morning, we drove down riot-torn streets that
could have been Beirut after a war or Mexico City after an earthquake.
Sadly and incredibly, it was Los Angeles. It was home.

We were searching for a place to unload our shovels and brooms
and get to work helping to clear the debris. Three friends from a mostly white suburb were with us. We pulled up beside a van with the words
"Normandie Church of Christ" painted on the side. "Do you know
where we go to help?" we yelled.

"Just follow us," they called back.

We all worked together to clear the rubble—blacks, whites, a
Latino gardening crew in matching green T-shirts. The stench was hor-
rible, and I often felt on the verge of tears, but it was good to be doing
something.

The Watts Riots the summer we came to Los Angeles had begun
when a white policeman pulled over a black motorist. This more recent
disturbance occurred because the policemen who beat a black man got
off, despite the fact that the whole country had watched the brutal
attack on television.

Despite promises of reform, during the almost three decades
between the two incidents, incomes in the area plummeted while
unemployment and police brutality soared. Neglect, injustice, racism,
poor education, and poverty had formed a tinderheap that needed only
a spark to leap into flame.

Violence is Everywhere

We prefer to think that, if we avoid certain neighborhoods that are commonly considered "bad," we can avoid violence. But violence is everywhere people are, because the potential for violence resides in the human heart—including yours and mine.

A few years later, when we moved to the Westside of Los Angeles, our families were relieved. They thought we were living in a safer place. None of our friends are afraid to visit us here.

Still, one morning a few months after we moved, I was working in the house when I heard a cry that froze my blood. As I started to the front of the house, I heard someone running down the driveway toward the back. I heard a crash and a scramble over our chain link fence. The person was in our backyard!

I peeked out the glass French doors and saw a black man in jeans and a white T-shirt. The front of his shirt was red with blood. I worked up the nerve to open the door. He was cowering beside the back porch.

"Are you O.K.?" I asked. It was obvious he wasn't. His face was puffy and bleeding. "Do you want me to call 9-1-1?"

"Please," he said hoarsely.

That told me he was the victim, not the perpetrator. I called the police. Then I went back to the door. "They'll be here soon," I said. I finally let him in the house and called the police again. They hadn't taken the first call seriously since the episode was over by the time I phoned.

While the man was cleaning up in the bathroom, I stuck my head out the bedroom window and asked our next-door neighbor, a retired policeman, to come over and sit with us. I was still uncomfortable being at home alone with a bloody black stranger, and both of us were frightened.

As we waited for the police to arrive, the man explained that he worked in the recording industry and had picked up the cash for his payroll. He hid the money in his car, then stopped to see a friend who lived in the apartment building next door to us. Apparently a couple of Hispanic men had followed him from the bank. Thinking he had the money with him, they pulled a gun and pistol-whipped him. When he yelled and ran, they jumped into their car and sped away.

Crime and violence aren't limited to low-income neighborhoods.

A few years later, we heard on the news that an employee of a local bookstore had been shot and killed. Our son worked at a bookstore, and when he came home from visiting friends, he called the store, only to discover that his manager, a long-time family friend, had been killed in a robbery.

"What kind of security do they have?" my husband asked.

"There is no security, Dad," Robert said in frustration. "It's a bookstore!"

He was right. Who would expect a robbery in a bookstore? But he was right in a more profound sense. There is no security anywhere. We can eat our vegetables, exercise, and not take unnecessary risks, but we can't escape death. "For the living know that they will die" (Eccles. 9:5).

We're all capable of violence

We're all going to die, but it's always a shock when it's by violent means. Maybe it shouldn't be. After all, violence is as old as Cain, who killed his brother Abel when his brother's offering was accepted and his wasn't (Genesis 4:1-16). And as shocking as violence may be, it's the result of very real emotions each of us has known.

Where does the violence that plagues our cities come from? The story of Cain and Abel suggests one set of sources: jealousy and unchecked competition. Jealousy can cause us to flare up at others, especially those we're closest to. Some of the most spiteful behavior is the result of family conflicts. Squabbles over inheritance, for instance, have created life-long breaches in relationships. After my grandfather's death, two of his daughters were so angry over the distribution of his estate that they went to their deaths refusing even to speak to each other. Competition enters a person's life with the birth of a brother or sister who is seen as a rival for the parents' love. The level of competitiveness can increase until we want to win, even at the expense of others.

Our current business environment, in which too many people are vying for too few jobs, constantly striving to move up, produce and succeed, increases tensions. And when pressures build that can't be expressed directly, they may erupt on innocent people around us. A man with an abusive boss comes home and abuses his wife. Laid-off workers return to their workplaces to wreak vengeance on whoever happens to be around. Stressed-out mothers slap or shake their children, too often resulting in injury or death, always in scars that can't be seen on the outside.

The Book of James suggests other sources of violence:

> Where do wars and fights come from among you? Do they not come from your desires for pleasure that war in your members? You lust and do not have. You murder and covet and do not obtain. You fight and war. Yet you do not have because you do not ask. You ask and do not receive, because you ask amiss, that you may spend it on your pleasures (James 4:1-3).

Selfishness and greed are another set of motivations for violence. These are the motives of much of the youth violence that plagues our streets. Desires, fed by a steady diet of advertising, have led young people to attack each other for cars, jewelry, drugs—even athletic shoes. Delayed gratification, working and saving to be able to purchase what we want, are becoming foreign concepts to many young—and not-so-young—people.

A constant barrage of advertising, conspicuous consumption, and misplaced values cause all of us to want things that aren't ours, that we can't really afford, and that might not even be good for us. It's easy to accept that constant litany of advertising, "You deserve it." If we feel we really do deserve something somebody else has, we may feel justified in taking it, and we certainly feel justified in coveting it.

Resentment can result when God doesn't meet our expectations, and resentment can easily grow into anger, a potentially dangerous emotion. As James put it, "Let every person be swift to hear, slow to speak, slow to wrath; for human wrath does not produce God's righteousness" (James 1:19-20).

And Jesus said:

> You have heard that it was said to those of old, "You shall not murder, and whoever murders will be in danger of the judgment." But I say to you that whoever is angry with his brother without a cause shall be in danger of the judgment. And whoever says to his brother, "Raca!" shall be in danger of the council. But whoever says, "You fool!" shall be in danger of hell fire (Matthew 5:21-22).

It's a passage I often remind myself of as I drive the streets of Los Angeles. When someone cuts in front of me or swerves across lanes of traffic, the temptation is great to question his or her intelligence. I've had to ask God many times to forgive me for a hasty "Idiot!" uttered in panic for my life. When we lose respect for our fellow human beings, refuse them the understanding we'd give ourselves in a similar situation, and allow anger to boil in our hearts, we are dangerously near to violence ourselves.

In fact, it's happened all too often. Road rage is a phenomenon of Los Angeles freeways in which frustration expresses itself in profanity, obscene gestures, even gunshots. I've seen people get so angry on the freeway that they've chased the offending driver and rearended his car.

We are our brothers' keepers

We may not know precisely why Cain killed his brother, but we do know that, when God confronted him, Cain responded with the age-old question, "Am I my brother's keeper?" It's a question that holds within it the solution to most of the violence that plagues our world—and especially our cities. The answer is that we are our brothers' keepers. We are responsible for each other—to respect each person as an individual with the same rights we have, including the right to live.

As Rick Marrs wrote, "In a world given to celebrating winners and discarding losers, Scripture calls us to be our *brother's keeper*. Through God's challenge to Cain, we hear God challenging us to forgo self-obsession and self-interest and love our brother!"[1]

"Because we humans are so prone to anger and aggression," Naomi Rosenblatt points out, "we need this story to remind us that all murders are fratricide within the human family—that we are all brothers and are ultimately consigned to each other's safekeeping."[2]

Our possessions belong to God

In addition to the question of human brotherhood, the incident of Cain killing Abel also raises the question of God's fatherhood. Why do we give gifts to God? Whether our material possessions, our praise, or our talents in service to others, our gifts are not to be just one side of a transaction, what we give so we can get something from him. Our gifts are a response to what God has done for us. In fact, all that we have is his. He has temporarily entrusted it to our keeping to use for his purposes. It's as Naomi Rosenblatt explains in *Wrestling with Angels*:

The first human offering to God underscores a sobering lesson in the art of giving: when we give, we should not expect to
get. Of course, when we feel we are giving our love, it's impossible not to want the gift reciprocated. And when this doesn't
happen, the spirit of our offering can quickly turn from love to
resentment to anger. It's unclear why God prefers Abel's offering over Cain's. Perhaps he is testing Cain's motives. Was Cain
actually offering thanks to God, or was he fishing for approval?[3]

As she continues discussing the story, Rosenblatt suggests one solution:

We have the capacity—indeed the obligation—to rein in our
anger and destructive drives. This moral imperative is a dis-
tinctly human task. Animals aren't subject to any such expectation. We don't expect compassion or understanding from lions
or tigers. But as human beings created in the image of God, we
are granted moral autonomy. Once we know the difference
between right and wrong, we are obliged to act on our best
instincts and restrain our worst ones.[4]

Our culture is violent

Our culture often portrays violence as the way problems are solved.
Popular culture glorifies the gunfighter, the gangster, the maverick police
officer who responds to frustration with violence. Domestic violence is
rampant, and we are the only first-world nation that practices capital
punishment. How do we expect our children to deal with problems
when that's the example we as parents and a society give them?

Many in the city have lost a sense of community. Cooperation has
given way to competition. We would rather fight for our own rights than
negotiate for the fair distribution of rights to everyone. "Do to others
what you would have them do to you" (Matthew 7:12) has become, "Do
others before they do you." If we cared as much about the opportunities
of other people's children to get a good education and a good job as we
do about our own, we wouldn't have neighborhoods where options are
so limited that dealing drugs is the first way some people think of to
make money.

Such altruism is a high ideal, but it's an ideal that can change the world. It may be impossible for human nature, but it isn't impossible for God as the Holy Spirit lives in us, changing us into his image.

Violence is the way some people express frustration over unmet needs, either physical or psychological. If someone wins our girlfriend or fires us from our job or even gives us a failing grade, violence often seems the reaction of choice. Like Paul, we need to learn to be content with whatever we have (Philippians 4:11-13). God is wise and loving. He gives us what we need. If we don't have something we want, maybe we don't need it—or maybe we don't need it yet. We may not be mature enough to handle it wisely or appreciate it properly.

We need to learn to handle frustration more effectively, to recognize that another person is as much a person as we are, a person with his or her own legitimate needs and desires. This ability to "feel with" another person is a characteristic of Jesus. The New Testament speaks often of the compassion he had for those he encountered (Matthew 9:36, 14:14, 15:32, 20:34; Mark 1:41, 8:2). Since compassion is a characteristic of Jesus, it should characterize us as we follow him.

Even if we haven't yet grown to compassion, God tells us, "Vengeance is mine, I will repay," (Romans 12:19). We don't have the right to play God—to decide who lives or dies—even who suffers. Each person is as valuable as any other. As Christians living in the city, perhaps that should be our message. Maybe we need to be more counter-cultural than we have been and not only resist but teach resistance to the get-even, get-yours, get-all-you-can attitude that surrounds us. But before we can teach it, we have to practice it.

One verse of scripture I learned to cling to when we lived in South Los Angeles was Hebrews 13:5-6:

> Let your conduct be without covetousness; be content with such things as you have. For he himself has said, "I will never leave you nor forsake you." So we may boldly say:

> "The Lord is my helper;
>   I will not fear.
> What can man do to me?"

We're not to want what we don't have, and we're not to be afraid despite the violence around us. We can trust God to know what we need and to take care of us in all circumstances. We don't have to worry about money. We don't have to fear other people.

God's people are called to trust him

An incident that occurred one November taught me more about trust than perhaps any other. As the month passed, I could tell that our paychecks would run out before Thanksgiving. We had taken turns with Frank's sister and her family, who were working in a children's home in Chino. We'd cook one year, and they would the next. I hadn't mentioned the problem, but as the month wore on, I began to realize that I should let them know we couldn't host them that year. In fact, we weren't going to make it through the month with food for ourselves.

Before I got around to calling, one of our neighbors called that her kids were down with the measles. Did I have some activity books she could borrow to keep them occupied? She'd be down to pick them up.

I was in the kids' room sorting through the activity books when I heard the doorbell ring. "That's Anita," I told Robert, who was just over two at the time. "Tell her to come in. I'll be right there."

I gathered the books and went into the living room. No Anita. Just Robert, standing in the middle of the floor, holding a pumpkin pie. "How sweet. I'll thank her when I take her the books." I was surprised that she hadn't waited long enough to take them herself.

"Look in the kitchen," Robert said. There were two grocery bags filled with a ham and a chicken, vegetables and fruit, brown-and-serve rolls, butter, milk, and a fruitcake! I stared in disbelief.

When I recovered enough to take the activity books down to Anita, she said, "You can keep the food for yourself or take it to your church to pass on to someone else. It's to pay you back for the food you gave us when Harold was off work." That had been three years earlier!

I thanked her profusely and explained our situation. There was no way Anita could know that we needed food right then—but God did. He provided our needs through a Catholic neighbor who was open to his leading.

Not that God always will protect us from harm. Bad things do happen to good people. God "sends rain on the just and on the unjust" (Matthew 5:45). That's one of the great challenges to our faith. There are two worlds—the physical and the spiritual. While we may not be exempt from the diseases, violence and bereavement that plague our physical lives, as God's children in the city, our true selves are secure with him.

It was a lesson we tried to teach through the "No to Violence" seminars we held in the mid-90s. When I was working for the Culver Palms Church of Christ as community outreach coordinator, we saw the seminars as a way to raise the profile of the church in the community while addressing a problem that was on many people's minds. We brought in special speakers and panelists to address such issues as the psychological roots of violence, violence in the schools, and racial violence. And we invited the community to consider the problem with us.

What can we, as people interested in urban ministry, do to counter the tendency to violence that we see around us?

1. *We can learn and demonstrate patience, faith and respect for others.* I've been growing in faith and learning greater respect for others, but patience has come harder to me. At one point in my life, I often found myself weaving down the freeway, trying to pass every car that was going slower than I wanted to. I felt hurried and harried and often arrived at my destination stressed and exhausted. Then one day, I tried an experiment. I noticed the particular car that was next to me, then did my usual weaving and passing until I reached my exit. Looking for the car, I saw that it was only one car length behind me. I had accomplished very little for all my efforts. That was when I started to slow down and "go with the flow."

2. *We can teach peace and responsibility.* Our children may know their rights, but not their responsibilities to others. We need to take advantage of every opportunity to encourage young people to promote peace, to slow down and enjoy the life God has given them, to honor others as people of equal worth. Violence in schools is touching ever younger children, and the children in our homes and churches need to learn better ways to cope.

3. *We can empty our houses of weapons.* When we first moved to Los Angeles, I brought my .22 rifle and 20-gauge shotgun with me. In Texas, I had enjoyed target practice in vacant fields. But in Los Angeles, living in married student housing units with paper-thin walls, I could imagine the damage that would result if one of them went off. I sent them back to my parents. Later, my daughter was in high school with a

young man who shot his girlfriend, though not fatally, in the face. His bedroom was full of guns and swords. If it hadn't been, he might have slapped her or socked her instead, with less grim consequences for both their lives.

4. *We, like Paul, can learn, teach and practice being content with what we have.* We need to resist the consumer mentality and constant barrage of advertising that can lead us to value things over people. We need to realize that covetousness is a sin against God as surely as breaking any of his other commands. It indicates a lack of trust that he knows and will provide our needs. We have our needs and wants confused to the extent that the household items listed as "needs" have multiplied a hundred times in recent years.

5. *We can offer and support programs that encourage positive relationships.* In the family, at school, at work, and in society in general, we can work for peace and reconciliation, promoting understanding across the barriers that divide us.

6. *We can teach and develop more effective ways of releasing tension.* A good, hard workout or a walk around the block, just stopping to think before we act, can give us a chance to cool off before we do or say something that can't be undone.

7. *And we can work to help all people have better opportunities for the advantages we want for ourselves and our children.* A livable wage, comfortable surroundings, and hope can go far in relieving the tensions and frustrations that can lead to violence.

Peace is a part of the gospel that we as Christ's children are to spread. As Paul said, "And he [Christ] came and preached peace to you who were afar off and to those who are near. For through him we both have access by one Spirit to the Father" (Ephesians 2:17-18). And, "now all things are of God, who has reconciled us to himself through Jesus Christ, and has given us the ministry of reconciliation, that is, that God was in Christ reconciling the world to himself, not imputing their trespasses to them, and has committed to us the word of reconciliation" (2 Corinthians 5:18-19). This reconciliation occurs in different directions— between us and God, between us and other people, and between us and ourselves.

God's vision of the church in the city is of a peaceable kingdom where lions lie down by lambs and a little child leads them (Isaiah 11:6-9). Let's pray and work toward the establishment of that kingdom in our cities.

God's vision for each of us as individuals is to be peacemakers who are blessed by him and are called his children (Matthew 5:9). Let's search our hearts and make love and forgiveness for our neighbors real in our lives.

God's vision for the city is one of peace and reconciliation. If we and those around us are reconciled and at peace with God, with ourselves and with each other, and if we spread that message of reconciliation to those near and those farther away, our city will be less likely to suffer the tragedies of crime and violence.

Questions for Discussion

1. Are crimes and violence increasing or decreasing in your city?

2. How can you overcome the fear of crime and violence?

3. What conditions feed crime and violence?

4. How can we, as Christians, promote peace and reconciliation in our cities?

5. How can we, as individuals, overcome resentments, greed, jealousy and selfishness in our own lives?

The Church

Chapter 5

The Church in the City

The Vermont Avenue Church of Christ began as a campus church, serving the administration, faculty and students of Pepperdine College. When Frank and I came to Los Angeles in 1965, it was mostly white, with one black elder, a few black deacons, and a scattering of black students. We got into town on a Saturday, and the next day we were worshipping at Vermont Avenue. We would be there for three decades.

When we arrived, we stayed with Frank's aunt and uncle, Helen and Norvel Young, until our apartment in married students' housing was ready. The Youngs were dedicated servants of God and of others. They had an international perspective and were comfortable with all sorts of people. Norvel was one of the elders at Vermont Avenue, so we went to worship with them the first Sunday we were in Los Angeles, intending to visit around before deciding on a home congregation.

The minister at the time was Gordon Teel, who spoke with a cultured accent, had a gruff, no-nonsense manner, and was one of the most loving people I'd ever known. Among the first people we met were Bill and Ruby Green. He'd been a classics professor at Berkeley and had come after his retirement there to teach Greek at Pepperdine. He had a great mind and a humble manner.

His wife Ruby involved me in my first ministry at Vermont Avenue when she asked me to walk out with her a little before services ended so we could meet visitors, most of whom sat toward the back and slipped out as soon as worship ended. It taught me while I was still an undergraduate that I was there to reach out and serve as a part of the church, not be served by the church. Surrounded by so many dynamic Christians, we saw no reason to search further for a church home.

Vermont Avenue was an exception among churches in Los Angeles, at least among predominantly white Churches of Christ, a loose affiliation of nondenominational churches. For the most part, they tended to be small, scattered, and somewhat in-turned. Our fellowship traditionally has been a rural movement. Even when members moved to the city, they tended to start small, rural-style churches plopped down in an urban environment. These churches became refuges for their members from the stresses of urban life, but they had little impact on their communities.

There are a number of differences between rural Christians and urbanites. Most people in rural churches know each other. They know and are comfortable with traditional church practices. They have the support network of established, often multi-generational, families.

On the other hand, urban people often are alienated. They may lack stable support networks and be unfamiliar with—or even question—traditional church practices. They have a consumer mentality and are accustomed to being able to pick and choose. Independent and opinionated, they aren't inclined to just "go along."

God's people are called to be like him

As a result of these differences, those of us in the church may feel threatened by the very people we are here to serve. We may adopt what J. Timothy Kauffman calls a "fortress mentality"[1] and hide behind fences, walls, and sophisticated alarm systems. So long as people come to us at the times and in the manner we've adopted, they are welcome. But we're at a loss for what to do with people who work Sunday mornings, who can't understand or are put off by what seem to them to be strange restrictions and means of determining how things are done, and by music styles and traditions that date from another century.

Even one of the things we are good at, one thing even most urbanites would admit they need—fellowship [Gr, *koinonia*]—can become part of the problem. We may be so happy to see each other on Sunday mornings and cling so closely together after the storms of the week that we make visitors at our services feel left out. Peter Wagner calls it "koinonitis" and describes it this way:

> Koinonitis is [an illness] caused by too much of a good thing.... Fellowship, by definition, involves interpersonal relationships. It happens when Christian believers get to know one another, to enjoy one another, and to care for one another. But as the disease develops, and *koinonia* becomes koinonitis, these interpersonal relationships become so deep and so mutually absorbing, they can provide the focal point for almost all church activity and involvement.[2]

Richard Gollings says, "'Koinonitis' (or the inflammation of the *koinonia*) involves an overemphasis on internalized fellowship to the point of a loss of interest in, and compassion for, those outside the group."[3]

A History of Service

Historically, Churches of Christ have not been known for their concern for outsiders, though there always have been notable exceptions. Both individual Christians and congregations have reached out to serve those around them, despite barriers. Some notable examples are the following:

David Lipscomb. David Lipscomb was an influential pioneer preacher and editor. According to Leonard Allen,

> In June of 1873 a deadly cholera epidemic struck Nashville, Tennessee. Dozens of people began dying daily, and on one particularly dark day—black Friday, June 20—at least 72 people died. The epidemic raged throughout the month of June, and when it was over more than a thousand people had succumbed to the disease—about one out of every forty residents of the city....
>
> The hardest hit were the poor and destitute, especially among the black population. At least 200 blacks died in the New Bethel Community in the southern part of the city.[4]

Most of the people with the resources to leave the city did so, but some remained to help. These included physicians, preachers, Catholic

nuns, and David Lipscomb and a group of young people from churches of Christ. Though physically weak at the time, Lipscomb risked his
life to distribute food and supplies, clean and feed destitute blacks in
their homes, and drive nuns in his buggy to minister to needs. "Every
individual, white or black, that dies from neglect and want of proper
food and nursing is a reproach to the professors of the Christian religion
in the vicinity of Nashville," he wrote.

As Allen points out, "For Lipscomb true Christianity was inextricably
wrapped up with regard for the poor. Indeed, his writings over fifty
years proclaim his deep conviction that ministry to the poor serves as a
fundamental identifying mark of the true church."[5]

Nashville Central Church of Christ. The Central Church of Christ in
Nashville was an early church that was noted for its benevolent outreach.

> In 1929-30, they found jobs for 590 people, provided free
> housing for 3,222, and served 6,046 free meals at noon. Two
> church-owned pick-up trucks delivered coal and groceries to
> the poor in downtown Nashville. A medical and dental clinic in
> the building served physical needs. Every day at noon, they held
> a preaching service. From 1925-29, they gave away 275,000
> pieces of religious literature. From 1925-45, they baptized over
> eight thousand people, about one a day.[6]

One of the ministers of the Central Church, E. H. Ijams, wrote the
following:

> "Churches of Christ, as I had observed them during the first
> quarter of the twentieth century, were commendably strong in
> doctrine, but were often very, very weak in good works....I
> came to feel that we could not get far in restoring the religion
> of the early Christians unless we learned to do a better job of
> uniting faith and works."[7]

Harold Shank summarized the qualities of the Central Church which
contributed to the success of its efforts[8]:

1. *They showed benevolence without any preaching strings attached.*
"No study was required to get help. No baptisms had to be in place

before purse strings were opened. No attendance at the noon meeting was required for the church pickup truck to bring more coal."

2. *They verbalized the gospel.* "The radio message of...God and His Son went into every part of the city. At noon every day and in the two Sunday assemblies, the church invited all to participate in a study of Scripture."

3. *Evangelism and benevolence were customized to the needs of the people.* "NCCC did not begin with specific doctrines of the church of Christ, but focused on the fundamental principles of the Christian faith: love, grace, and mercy. As people became more interested, they were taught how to become Christians and the specific views of the church."

Madison Church of Christ. A more recent example is the Madison Church of Christ, under its dynamic minister, Ira North. North said,

> It is my considered judgment that the weakest link in the pro-
> gram of most congregations is in the area of benevolence....
> There is a mystery in an active, wide-awake benevolent pro-
> gram that I cannot explain, but I have seen the results with my
> own eyes. It just seems that when a congregation gets involved
> in a program of benevolence that God opens the windows of
> heaven and the fountains of the deep and pours out his blessings.[9]

In 1971, 9,360 hot meals were prepared and delivered through Madison's Meals on Wheels. In addition to Meals on Wheels, the "Care 'N' Share" Center housed a food room, used clothing and a sewing room. A pickup truck used to gather furniture had printed on its side, "Dealers in faith, hope and love."[10]

In 1975, 1,853 new items of clothing were made and 31,635 used items given to those in need. In 1967, a total of 220 family units were served by the furniture room. From 1960-67, seven cottages were built, initiating Madison Children's Home. Over one thousand children were cared for in 25 years of operation. The church also sponsored homes for victims of domestic violence and for the elderly.[11]

"It is surprising how much the Bible has to say about helping the poor, the lowly, the homeless, the helpless, the aged, and the widows," North said. "The world sees the fine buildings put up in Christendom. Millions of dollars are invested in sticks and stones and bricks, and yet all too little is done for the poor." He pointed out that the budget of the average church indicates that it generally is the church's weakest area of ministry.

Current Efforts. Currently, efforts at combining the words of the gospel with good works of service are expanding. Examples include HopeWorks in Memphis, Tennessee; Central Dallas Ministries in Dallas, Texas; Impact in Houston, Texas; PUMP in Portland, Oregon; as well as works in Birmingham, Alabama; Lubbock, Texas; Chicago, New York and Detroit.

God's people in the city have never been called to separate ourselves from those around us. Rebecca Pippert wrote that Jesus is our example of living God's message. Then she tells us the qualities that made him such an effective communicator:

> Jesus told us that as the Father sent him into the world, so he is sending us (John 17:18). How then did the Father send him? Essentially he became one of us. The Word became flesh (John 1:14). God didn't send a telegram or shower evangelistic Bible study books from heaven or drop a million bumper stickers from the sky saying, "Smile, Jesus loves you." He sent a man, his Son, to communicate the message. His strategy hasn't changed. He still sends men and women—before he sends tracts and techniques—to change the world....
>
> In Jesus, then, we have our model for how to relate to the world, and it is a model of openness and identification....We must learn then to relate transparently and genuinely to others because that is God's style of relating to us....
>
> How can we relate to people in a way that will change the world? Jesus did it in two ways: by his radical identification with men and women, and by his radical difference."[12]

We need to identify with the people around us like Jesus did while retaining our distinctive identity as children of God. We are to be salt and light, influencing people for Christ. As Jesus said in the Sermon on the Mount, "You are the salt of the earth. But if the salt loses its saltiness how can it be made salty again? It is no longer good for anything except to be thrown out and trampled by men" (Matthew 5:13).

Just as useless is the salt that never comes in contact with the substance it is intended to preserve or flavor. Generally, the longer a person has been a Christian, the fewer non-Christian friends he or she has. We often consider this a point of pride, but it should condemn us. The only Christians with a considerable number of non-Christian friends are new converts. We're leaving our newest, weakest members to be salt while those of us who are more mature huddle in the saltshaker.

Even church programs can compete with Jesus' call to impact those around us. Most churches have enough activities aimed at us and ours to keep us busy inside the church building and in each others' houses all the time we have available beyond work, eating, sleeping, and recreational activities.

Other things that are good in themselves, indeed, even required, can become barriers to our reaching out to others. For instance, the call to holiness, to separation from the world, can be distorted to the extent that we avoid those who most need our ministry. God calls us to be in the world, but not of it (John 17:11, 14-16). How can we learn to care about people beyond ourselves and our families and friends? How can we develop God's love for the world, a love that does good and benefits others?

At one point, when we were living in the South Bay and commuting back to the Vermont Avenue Church, I became convicted by the fact that almost all of my friends were Christians. I set out consciously to make more non-Christian friends. Having written short stories and started work on a novel, I felt writing was a good interest to try to share. I signed up for a fiction writing class at the local junior college. At break time, a few of us started having coffee together under umbrellas outside our building. We became the nucleus of a writer's workshop that met together for two decades and created lasting friendships.

Cathi, Dale, Mike, Dan, Renee, and I were the beginning. Marla, Melissa, Andi, and Luis were among those who joined us later. We read and critiqued each other's work and went on retreats together. Most of the members of the group came to worship with me or participated in church activities at one point or another. Dale became a minister, others became more spiritually oriented, Luis' family began attending services at Vermont regularly, and Melissa was baptized years later and became a part of the Culver Palms Church. Friendship evangelism is an effective form of urban ministry.

God's people are called to engage the world

When the Israelites, God's people in the Old Testament, were over-thrown by the Babylonians, many were exiled to Babylon and other nations the Babylonians had conquered. The prophet Jeremiah remained in Jerusalem with a remnant of God's people. Jeremiah was a faithful messenger from God in those bad times. He repeatedly warned the people not to rebel against Babylon or try to escape into Egypt. His message was seldom what the people wanted to hear.

In Jeremiah 29, Jeremiah again addressed the exiles. They weren't too pleased with that message, either. They wanted him to say that they soon would be returning to Jerusalem, and they were ready to live as exiles in their new homes, waiting for that day to come. But Jeremiah told them to

> Build houses and dwell in them; plant gardens and eat of their fruit. Take wives and beget sons and daughters; and take wives for your sons and give your daughters to husbands, so that they may bear sons and daughters—that you may be increased there and not diminished. And seek the peace of the city where I have caused you to be carried away captive, and pray to the Lord for it; for in its peace you will have peace (Jeremiah 29:5-7).

Robert C. Linthicum in his book *City of God, City of Satan: a Biblical Theology of the Urban Church*, asks,

> Why are you in the city in which you live? You may have been born there. You may have decided to move there. You may be in that city because you took a job there or have built a career there. You may be in that city because your spouse or a loved one is there. You may have come to that city to be edu-cated or to retire there. But none of those reasons are why you actually live in that city. Those are simply the circumstances God has used to bring you there.
>
> Why are you in the city in which you find yourself? You are there, Jeremiah suggests, for one reason and one reason alone. You are in your city because God has called you there. You are in your city by God's design, by God's will. Whether God's

plans for you in that city turn out to be plans for your peace and not for your disaster depend on whether you can see yourself as being called by God into your city, and then whether you can seek to live faithfully according to that call.[13]

Too many Christians in the city today live there as if in exile. Their hearts and minds are on their previous homes, and they never become a wholehearted part of the city. Many come to find work and, as soon as they retire, or even have saved enough money, they go back where they came from.

Jeremiah's advice is just as true for these self-imposed "exiles" as it was for the exiles in Babylon. We should

- *participate* in the life of the city.
- seek the *peace* of the city.
- *pray* for the city.
- be God's *presence* in the city.

God's people are called to participate in the life of the city

Soon after we moved out of married student housing into our house on 79th Street across from the campus, we invited the people on our block for a barbecue. We were surprised to find ourselves introducing people to each other who had lived on the same block for years. We became parts of each others' lives—helping one neighbor after her husband died, catching one neighbor's son robbing another neighbor's house, helping the children next door with their homework, and generally sharing good times and bad.

God's people are called to seek the peace of the city

The Wednesday evening class I taught at Vermont Avenue was a combined Bible class and schoolroom. Every lesson was a Bible lesson, but we read from simplified versions of the Bible so I could help the children learn to read. Bible numbers were translated into math problems, and maps were plentiful. Old National Geographic magazines illustrated the fact that Bible stories took place in real places at real times. A few children became more interested in school when they realized that what they learned there wasn't just odd facts in a vacuum, but information that could be applied in other contexts.

Vacation Bible School centered around themes, and eventually I began using similar themes for our regular classes, creating environments that exposed the children to places they hadn't been. In one unit we "camped in the woods," pitching a tent in a stand of artificial Christmas trees surrounded by rocks and artificial plants, birds—even plastic snakes and bugs. A circle of rocks with sticks inside became our "campfire." We'd sit on the floor around it and talk and pray about the problems of the week. I was surprised at the way even teenagers opened up in our campfire devotions. Some city children just need someone to listen.

Another class used sea creatures to illustrate God's hidden nature. At the end of that unit, members of the English and Spanish congregations carpooled down to Cabrillo Beach Marine Museum in San Pedro. It was thrilling to see inner city children rushing from one exhibit to another, shouting, "That's a starfish," "There's a sea urchin." "Look, an octopus. See the suckers on his tentacles? One, two, three….Yeah, there's eight all right."

Our daughter Kathy grew up in South Los Angeles, and her brother Robert was born there. Kathy grew up, first with children of all races whose parents were connected with Pepperdine, and then, when the college left, with African-American children in the neighborhood. She attended Normandie Christian School, a school founded by the Normandie Church of Christ, a large and active black church in the area. She played with the children on our block.

We lived in walking distance of the Vermont Avenue building, but every Wednesday night for a couple of years, we made a circuit of surrounding neighborhoods, filling our little Opel station wagon with children of all ages—mostly African-American children to take to Bible classes at Vermont Avenue.

God's people are called to pray for the city

How often do you pray for your city? How often do you ask God to give it peace and prosperity, because you identify so completely with it that you know that your good depends on its good?

In all the places we've lived, I've had regular devotions—mostly in the mornings, including reading the Bible and a devotional book, writing in my journal and praying. Sometimes it's been more regular than others, sometimes it's varied in format, but always it has included prayer—for the city, for the church in the city, and for individuals, both in and out of the church, who have special needs.

God's people are called to be his presence in the city

As children of God, we are never to be just "marking time." We're always to be serving God and other people—to be God's presence in our city.

> Your task in Babylon, the prophet said, is not to dream of the "good old days" nor yearn for your return to the Promised Land. Your task is to get on with your life in that place in which God has placed you right here and now....
>
> Be what you are—God's living presence in the city...The presence of godly people in the city will save it from destruction.
>
> * * * * *
>
> Jeremiah advises the Israelite exiles in Babylon to live into God's urban call to them by becoming a godly presence in their adopted city....God says the same to God's people today. Whatever the circumstances might be that have brought you to your city, what God most wants out of you as a Christian in that city is to live fully into your circumstances.
>
> Buy a house or rent an apartment, God instructs you and me. Find your vocation and enter into your city's economics. Buy and sell. Give and take. Love your neighborhood; commit yourself to its people. Laugh and cry with them. Celebrate and mourn with them. Make an investment of yourself and your family in your city.[14]

God's people may be a part of the problem

Why do we so often fail to engage the city we're a part of?

One problem may be our definition of the church. If we view the church solely as a worshipping society or a place to have our needs met, we won't be involved in God's mission of saving the lost and serving those around us. Another problem may be a fear of the social gospel—of an unreal dichotomy between saving souls and serving people.

If we emphasize head knowledge instead of heart knowledge, we may be able to recite scripture but have trouble living sacrificial, Christlike lives. It's like the discussion we had when we were planning our out-reach ministry at Culver Palms. One man suggested that we hand out Bible questions to people coming to seek our help. I didn't understand. Bible questions for people who might or might not be Christians? "What kind of questions do you have in mind?" I asked.

"Oh, simple questions," he replied, "like 'who built the ark?'"

We've done that, haven't we, even in Bible classes—tested people on their Bible knowledge instead of showing them Jesus? made Bible knowledge, not submission to Christ, the standard?

Another dichotomy that may hinder our churches' reflecting Christ to the world is the dichotomy between grace and works. With good reason, we've come to appreciate God's grace and to realize that we can't earn salvation. That doesn't mean, however, that we shouldn't do anything. We still do good deeds; it's just that our motivation has changed. We do good, not to save ourselves, because that's impossible, but out of gratitude for what God has done for us through Christ. Because of his sacrificial sharing with us, we want to share our gifts with others.

In the past few years, politics has entered in. I remember when Christians didn't get into politics at church. Christians might be Democrats or Republicans, progressives or conservatives. That was their business, related to their earthly citizenship, not their heavenly. Political views were never expressed from the pulpit.

In the past few years, though, at least in Los Angeles, some of our churches have bought into the larger evangelical movement to the point where Christian has come to be equated with politically conservative. Some have grown hostile in their opposition to social issues they aren't inclined to take part in, like homosexuality and abortion. It's easier to judge something we don't do than to consider our own shortcomings.

The fact that some have emphasized these issues while neglecting to love those who disagree with them has caused many non-Christians to see us as hateful and mean-spirited. It's a far cry from Jesus, who was known as the friend of sinners. We learn to feel strongly about an issue without behaving in an un-Christian manner.

Fear and middle-class prejudices can cause us to be less effective in engaging the city than we might be. We tend to look at large segments of the city as either good and bad. There are places where we don't drive—at least at night. Thus, we end up with white-collar criminals who defraud widows and retirees of millions of dollars living in "good" neighborhoods while minority youth, who rip off jewelry or sports shoes, are consigned to "bad" neighborhoods. Our sense of morality—of what really is good and bad—suffers as a result.

As Jackie Warmsley points out in "A Little Story about Jumping,"

> After all, if we can succeed in branding our world "good," and the world of the unfortunate and disadvantaged "bad," we can stay apart rather than being part of the solution.
>
> Jesus went to the people. Somehow, churches declared that if people were good, they would come to him.[15]

And that's what it ultimately comes down to, isn't it? Sin. We fail to engage the city because we're selfish, proud, greedy, impatient, and generally just don't care enough about other people. We lack kindness, servanthood, and time. We want to do what we want to do. It's far from the attitude of Jesus.

Being Christ's Body

How can we truly be Christ's body, his representatives in a city that at times may frighten, sadden, and even disgust us? How can we expand our fellowship to reach out to those who are different from ourselves? What are some concrete ways we can participate in the life of the city, seek its peace, pray for it and be God's presence in it?

Do we need a broader definition of what the church is and does? Can we avoid creating false dichotomies that interfere with the commission Jesus gave us to teach and make disciples?

How can we avoid confusing our earthly and our heavenly citizenship? How can we stop judging the various parts of the city by our own comfort level? How can we overcome the sins that keep us from responding to the needs of those around us? What can we do to make our churches, and ourselves, reflect more of Jesus' loving, forgiving, sacrificial nature?

God's vision for the city intimately involves our being a people who live like Jesus did, who participate in the life of the city, seek the peace of the city, pray for the city, and demonstrate his presence by incarnating his qualities of openness and identification, bringing healing and help to those around us. Let's try to catch that vision and find practical ways to live it in our daily lives.

Questions for Discussion

1. How can your congregation have a warm and loving fellowship that's still open to outsiders?

2. How effective is your congregation at uniting faith and works? What does the church's budget indicate about the importance of helping people?

3. How can you as Christians become salt and light to attract more people?

4. What can you as an individual do to make more non-Christian friends with the aim of leading them to Christ?

5. How can you participate more actively in the life of your city?

Chapter 6

Building Bridges

For thirty years, I served as a part of the Vermont Avenue Church in South Los Angeles. Then, in 1994, I became a part of the Culver Palms Church on the Westside. It was a wrenching move, and for months I sat in worship, overwhelmed by the size of the building, the number of people worshipping there, and the beauty and professionalism of all that was done. Would I ever fit in? Would I ever get to know all these people? Would I ever cease to feel intimidated?

Some 300-400 people meet on Sunday mornings to worship God at Culver Palms. Not a huge congregation compared with the church in many places, but large to me after worshipping with a struggling church that had dropped below 50 in the English-speaking services. After living and serving for decades in the city, I again felt like a lost child from a small town.

Not long after I came to Culver Palms, I was employed to do community outreach. And, not long after I was hired, our minister asked me what I saw myself doing in five years. I had designed a curriculum for a weekend seminar that I called "Community Connections" and had taught it in several churches. This was my chance to put its principles into practice. What would the practical results be? I didn't have a clue—and I told him so.

"You may not know now, when you're just starting," he said, "but you'd better have an answer in six months."

Six months later, I did have an answer to his question, but even that wasn't close to what eventually happened. Six months later, I had only begun to catch God's vision for his people's potential for outreach into this part of Los Angeles. It was three years later, as a student at Fuller Seminary, that I finally wrote a paper[1] setting out that vision as I was able to glimpse it:

Imagine an island surrounded, not by water, but by a large city, like the Île de la Cité in the Seine, with Paris all around. That's what the church is like. The apostle Peter says that we as the church are "a chosen people, a royal priesthood, a holy nation, a people belonging to God, that you may declare the praises of him who called you out of darkness into his wonderful light" (1 Peter 2:9).

We are priests, and the word for priest, *pontifex*, is Latin for "bridge-builder." We are called to build bridges between the island and the city surrounding it, between God's people and those around us who don't know Christ. The point is to get as many people as possible onto the island, and amazingly, it can hold as many as choose to come. According to Robert Kolb,

> God has made his people so that we might build a bridge between the revelation of his saving will for us, his recreating Word, and the people of our day and our society. He has entrusted his Word to us, as he gives it in the Scriptures which he breathed and in which he has set the authoritative form of his Word, so that we might proclaim it and apply it to the people in our culture in terms which effectively translate that Word for them.[2]

For maximum efficacy at our task, I would suggest that we need to build as many bridges as possible—footbridges, auto bridges, bridges capable of carrying heavy trucks and buses, even railroad bridges and tunnels. If the job is to get the people of the city onto the island, we need to use as many means as possible to get them there.

And the traffic has to flow both ways. We need to leave our island and go where the people are so we can give them the message of God's saving grace and encourage them to come to his island.

Everyone needs forgiveness and reconciliation—not only the homeless person shuffling down the alley rummaging through trash cans, but high-stakes executives, harried managers, working moms whose lives are a perpetual balancing act of demands, and retail clerks who go home to empty apartments.

The challenge to urban churches is to devise strategies to reach people who are hurting but don't know where to turn, who are hungry but don't know how to be filled, who need to be reached at a more basic level than we're accustomed to. Rather than asking "Who built the ark?" we may need to ask, "Do you believe in God?" "Do you believe in Jesus Christ?" "Do you know anything about the Bible?" "Would you like to learn?" Or even, "I think you'd enjoy getting to know one or two of the people I worship with. Why not come with me some Sunday morning, and I'll introduce you."

Building through images: acceptance

What is the first thing people think about when they hear the name of the church? A building? A program? A person they know who worships there? Do they even know the church exists?

The Culver Palms Church of Christ meets on Venice Boulevard, a major artery that stretches from downtown Los Angeles west to Venice Beach. The church building is located just southeast of the intersection of the 405 freeway and the 10, the busiest freeway intersection in the county. It was identified by the International Church of Christ as the ideal place for a church planting. We were already there.

The church had been meeting for sixty years at the line between Culver City and the Palms district of Los Angeles. Ten years ago, the congregation constructed a new building that reflected the Spanish heritage of Southern California with bold arches and tile roofs. Its modern lines indicate the forward-looking vision of the congregation. The only problem was that, though the building is located on Venice Boulevard, it fronts on a tiny, residential side street that dead-ends a block away. The "face" presented to most people is a parking lot and the side of the building. Since I came to Culver Palms, I've wanted to pick up that building and turn it 90 degrees to face Venice Boulevard.

We needed to do a lot more to let people know who and where we were. Advertising was part of the solution. Institutional advertising was never intended to sell products. As George Barna points out,

Advertising may effectively inform people of the existence of the church and may also position the church in a positive light. Advertising, however, does not motivate people to change their existing behavioral pattern to include church attendance or embrace Christ as their Savior.[3]

Effective institutional advertising creates a climate of acceptance, helps distinguish us from nearby Culver Palms United Methodist Church, creates a sense of the church as a solid part of the community, and allows us to state our distinct message in our own distinct way.

Two strengths of our church fellowship mentioned most frequently on the first impression cards enclosed in letters from the minister to first-time visitors are its friendliness and the racial and ethnic diversity of its membership. Our greatest attraction for those who may not have developed a spiritual hunger is our people, so I designed an advertising campaign called "Faces," which featured various members of the congregation.

A committee of artists, writers, photographers and computer experts designed a simple logo for the church. Then we prepared a brochure to introduce the church to the community. "The Faces of Culver Palms" depicts attractive and smiling people of all ages and races engaged in worship, Bible study, and fellowship.

Extensive advertising in the yellow pages featured the various language groups that meet at the building and the care groups meeting in homes in various parts of the city through the week. They attract both non-Christians from the area and Christians who have not yet found a church home.

A series of ads in a local newspaper featured individuals and families with interesting jobs or hobbies. Each was introduced with a photo showing the person engaged in that pursuit, together with an identifying caption. A brief quote written by the person related that job or interest to his or her faith.

An African-American medical biologist from UCLA was pictured in a lab coat among sophisticated lab equipment under the headline, "Why would a scientist believe in God?" In three simple sentences, he explained that the precision and design of nature strengthened his faith. The second ad depicted an artist in her studio. "What inspires an artist to create beauty?" was the question, and the artist answered with a brief story of her overwhelming gratitude to God for the glory of a field of poppies at dawn.

Then there was the couple whose hobby was cooking. She trained at Maxim's in Paris, and he grew up in New Orleans. In their photo, she was holding a souffle fresh from the oven, and he was slipping around to douse it with hot sauce as their two-year-old looked on in shocked delight. "How do you add spice to a marriage?" read the headline that introduced their statement of the central role of Christian principles in the success of their relationship.

The next year's budget was presented in a booklet on Worship, Evangelism, Discipleship and Outreach, the "WE DO" book, which featured pictures of people engaged in various activities. But images are not enough. There must be substance behind them.

Building through presence: participation

One of the first ways we create substance is through presence evangelism. According to Fuller professor Eddie Gibbs, who taught my class on "Church Growth through Effective Evangelism," presence evangelism "signifies being present in the world to listen, identify needs, and demonstrate a willingness to serve."[4]

Considering these points one at a time, we need to learn to *listen*. As a Christian, my tendency has always been to talk. I'm a problem solver, and I often listen just long enough to identify the problem so I can offer good advice. Too often that means an easy solution, and easy solutions seldom get to the heart of the matter. People's hearts are hurting, and only by really listening, listening long and hard, can we hear the message behind the words.

Only when we've heard the message can we truly *identify needs*. Some needs are easier to identify than others. We may survey our neighborhood and discover a need for child care. That's clear enough. If mothers are working—and many mothers in the city, both married and single, have to work to buy groceries, pay the rent, and keep gas in the car—they need to know that their children are safe and well cared for.

But as we continue to listen without being too quick to offer advice, we may discover that their need for child care, though very real, is not as great as their need for security, friendship, or self-esteem.

Then and only then are we able to *demonstrate a willingness to serve*. It helps people just to "get a load off their mind," but it helps even more when we're able to offer a more tangible solution. That might involve setting up a childcare center, instituting a Neighborhood Watch program, or just being a friend.

Not long after I was hired by the Culver Palms church, my husband and I moved into the area. Though the twenty-minute drive from the South Bay wasn't a long commute by local standards, I felt the need to be a part of the community I was trying to serve. For the past nine years, we've lived just blocks from the church building.

For a strategic plan, I adopted the three overlapping circles, like three Olympic rings, developed by Charles Van Engen and Jude Tiersma at Fuller Seminary.[5]

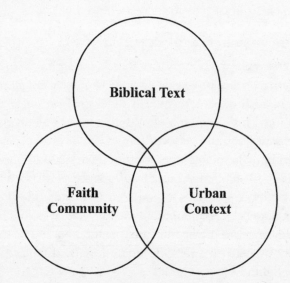

The rings are arranged in a pyramid, with the top one representing the Biblical text, and the lower two, the Faith Community and the Urban Context. I had known the concept intuitively before I went to Fuller, but it helped to have it diagrammed in a form that was easy to comprehend. To be a bridge-builder between the church and its community, I needed to study the Word, to study the church, and to study the community.

Van Engen explains that the rings illustrate three areas of the theology of mission. "Theology of missions is *theology* (circle A above), because fundamentally it involves reflection about God. It seeks to understand God's mission, God's intentions and purpose, God's use of human instruments in God's mission, and God's working through people in God's world...."

Second, he tells us, theology of mission is theology *of* (circle B). It is an applied theology similar to pastoral or practical theology. This type of theological reflection focuses on a set of particular issues—those concerning the church's mission.

Finally, theology of mission is specifically oriented toward and for *mission* (circle C). This form of theology can't restrict itself to reflection alone. It "draws its incarnational nature from the ministry of Jesus, and always happens in a specific time and place." There's a "strong dialectical tension between seeing people's faces and seeing those faces in their urbanized context."[6]

Text, Faith Community, and Urban Context in the Early Church

We see the three arenas of Text, Faith Community, and Urban Context in tension from the very beginning of the church. The fledgling fellowship "continued steadfastly in the apostles' doctrine and fellowship, in the breaking of bread, and in prayers....So continuing daily with one accord in the temple, and breaking bread from house to house, they ate their food with gladness and simplicity of heart, praising God and having favor with all the people. And the Lord added to the church daily those who were being saved" (Acts 2:42-47).

The growth of the early church was built firmly on the Word and the communal life of the first Christians. But they never cut themselves off from the context of the city of Jerusalem. They continued meeting in the temple, they enjoyed the favor of those around them, and others were added to their numbers daily.

Still, it wasn't long before tensions grew (Acts 3:1-8, 4:13-31). Peter and John, having healed a lame beggar at the gate of the temple, used the occasion to preach to the people who gathered, telling them about God and Jesus, the source of their healing power. The offended authorities arrested Peter and John and warned them not to preach about Jesus. "Whether it is right in the sight of God to listen to you more than to God, you judge," the two apostles told them. "For we cannot but speak the things which we have seen and heard" (Acts 4:19-20). The authorities couldn't come up with a way to punish the apostles, because the people "all glorified God for what had been done" (4:21), so they released them. Peter and John prayed for even greater boldness.

Those who minister to the city—and this means all urban Christians, not just paid personnel—need to study their community and find ways to reach out to local residents, gain favor with them, and cause them to glorify God as well.

The circles overlap because urban life and ministry occur in all three arenas at once. Of course, studying the Word has been a continuing project since I was a child, but I needed to study it more systematically as it applies to urban ministry. That was why I enrolled at Fuller. And I know the Church like I know my biological family, but I needed more study there as well.

The first step in developing such a strategy is research. *I needed to determine the gifts, interests and abilities that existed in the congregation.* First, I put together focus groups to discover what attracted the people to this particular fellowship, what they gained from their association with it, and what they felt they could contribute. Then I devised a list of thirty distinct ministries—from leading singing to keeping the nursery to decorating for potlucks—for people to participate in. Finally, I put together classes on discovering and using our spiritual gifts and on reaching out to the community.

There's a sound theological basis for such an approach. The theology of gifts suggests that each of us has something valuable to offer, some special gift from God that can direct and inform our service. And the theology of the priesthood of believers states that each of us as Christians is called to proclaim Christ, to teach others, to worship, love, witness and serve.

But I soon realized that my weakness, as well as the weakness of most of our urban churches, was that we don't give much attention to the city surrounding us except to take advantage of the attractions it offers.

I needed to learn more about the community around us before I could determine its needs and interests. Recognizing that I needed to know more about my part of the city than just the businesses to frequent and the tourist and entertainment destinations, I joined the Culver City Chamber of Commerce, the Healthy Start Collaborative at our local school district, and the executive board of the local service planning area of the County Children's Planning Council (SPA5). I attended meetings and met civic leaders. I read publications and census reports to try to understand the demographics of the area.

What are some distinct characteristics of urban life?[7]

1. Isolation is endemic to the city. This may sound strange, considering the crowds and bustle. But the very size of a city like Los Angeles, the sheer number of people who live here, make it hard to form deep and lasting friendships. Matt Soper, who was our minister when I came to Culver Palms, started the Welcome ministry with friendly people stationed at the door and at the welcome table in the foyer to be sure that everyone who comes receives a friendly greeting and signs the welcome book so they can receive a personalized letter.

2. More than a third of the adults in urban areas are single. These single adults, with or without children, often live far from their extended families and the support systems they provide. Realizing this, I started a care group for young singles that within three years grew from a handful to 25 people.

3. An increasing number of city dwellers are international—people from varied nations and cultures whose attitudes and practices may puzzle and even offend us. Congregations worshipping in Spanish, Korean, and Chinese meet in our building and people from every continent attend our English-speaking services.

4. Today's urban dwellers are suspicious of religion and resistant to intrusive efforts to evangelize. While they may take part in activities they perceive as helpful to themselves and their families, they may not be in the habit of committing to much of anything. There was a need for each of us to practice friendship evangelism, making friends outside of church and inviting those friends to visit with us. Our regular Friends Day made that easy.

5. They're mobile and may not remain in the area long. They're busy and distracted—with jobs and personal lives and all the attractions the city offers. We need to recognize the urgency of reaching and involving people while they're with us.

About this time, the elders did a congregational survey, and I was pleased to discover that the demographics of the congregation reflected those of our community, except for a slightly higher educational level among church members.

About a quarter of local and church households are headed by single mothers. Single mothers may feel lonely, and because women still earn significantly less, on average, than men, single mothers could have significant financial needs.

Also, unlike many congregations, ours had almost as many singles as married members, also a reflection of the makeup of the community. I taught a Bible class called "Women Who Come to Church Alone" about single women in scripture who were active servants of God. It was designed to encourage single women to participate in the work of the church.

Only after we had studied the church and the community could we devise programs that used the gifts of Christians to meet needs in the community. It's important not just to help, though Jesus helped and healed many, but to be Christ in the world, to make connections, to put a face on the church.

Too many of us have been content with business as usual—opening the doors each Sunday and allowing anyone who comes of their own initiative to join us. But we needed a specific strategy, a concerted effort to build excitement, to let people know we were here.

Most people today don't care about our doctrinal stand. They want to know what we have to offer them. And what we have to offer are relationships, knowledge, peace, and a sense of self-worth. Of course, all these blessings flow from our lives in Christ, and that fact must be communicated, but it may not be the first point of contact.

Now we were ready to invite our neighbors to participate in our events, classes and worship periods. Not everyone responded, but many did. Our responsibility was to sow the seeds, make contacts, live Christ's love, and trust him for the increase.

The only thing left that could get in the way of such a strategy was our own human nature:[8]

- *Selfishness.* Human beings are basically selfish. It's easy to apply all our energies "in-house," to limit our ministries to those benefiting us and ours.
- *Lethargy.* Urban dwellers—Christian and non-Christian alike— have many demands on our time and energy. We often feel like just coming home and collapsing when the work day is done.

- *Comfort.* People are conservative. Many become satisfied with the status quo and fear outreach because of the changes it might bring in the size, makeup, and orientation of the church.
- *Fear.* Many Christians see the world as a threat, not an opportunity. They see Satan, not God, as victorious.

In the face of such obstacles, we need to surrender ourselves to Jesus to do his work, rely on his strength and wisdom and not our own, incarnate Christ by showing love for each other and the world, reach beyond our comfort zones, be creative, break the mold of old thought patterns and approaches, and meet people where they are.

Urban ministry isn't just opening a food pantry or handing out secondhand clothes, though it may involve those methods. It's joining the PTA and hosting a Business Person's Prayer Breakfast. It's living in an apartment building and inviting your neighbors to a small group Bible study. It's mobilizing artists and actors, scientists and marketers, educators and lawyers, carpenters and gardeners in the church to share their talents and reach out to those they live and work with.

In fact, it's mostly about *connections*—raising the profile of the church in the city and creating an awareness that we exist, that we have something to offer, that we care, and that all are encouraged to participate.

One of our outreach efforts was a followup to Vacation Bible School offering parenting classes to the parents of children who had attended.

We hosted a coffeehouse for singles, complete with little round tables with red and white cloths, strings of tiny clear lights, cappuccino and biscotti selections printed on a blackboard, live entertainment and a display of paintings and photos by artists from the congregation. The only reference to Christianity was the testimony of one of the young singles.

Finally, as a gesture to the local film industry, we taught a Bible class on the life of Jesus illustrated with clips from movies about his life. Each week featured a different event in Jesus' life as envisioned by three different film directors. Then we read and discussed the relevant scripture and the significance of similarities and differences in the portrayals.

How can we sustain our enthusiasm to reach people who may be indifferent, thoughtless, wounding, even hostile? How can we avoid being paralyzed by the magnitude of the task and discouraged by its frustrations? How can we serve consistently, not jumping from one fad to another?

First, we need to realize that God *can* use us to impact the city, "because the one who is in [us] is greater than the one who is in the world" (1 John 4:4). We need to live prayerfully in his presence, relying on him for wisdom. We need to live by faith, not fear, in the face of the challenge. As Henri Nouwen said, "For the future of Christian leadership, it is of vital importance to reclaim the mystical aspect of theology, so that every word spoken, every advice given, and every strategy developed can come from a heart that knows God intimately."9 Without intimate relationship with God, what do we have to offer our world?

Second, we have to grow in love and learn to accept people with different standards without being shocked or swayed or drawn into their activities. In other words, we need to love sinners, remembering that that's what Jesus did for all of us.

Third, we need to look at the life and ministry of Jesus. How did he relate to the people around him? When Jesus was on this earth, he taught people by word and example, he met needs, and he empowered people to meet their own needs.

How do we reach out with the Gospel to the lonely, alienated, restless people of our city?

1. We need to catch their attention, to make them aware of our existence.

2. We need to be warm and friendly as individuals and open and caring as a Christian family. This atmosphere may be hard to maintain, because Christians in the city are subject to the pressures that affect everybody else. We're busy and distracted, and we may be reluctant to invest in friendships that may not last.

3. We need to offer creative programs that attract the people in our community. Most won't come just because we open the doors and worship God every week. Too many other people do the same. There are many competing voices, and urban dwellers are adept at tuning out those who don't offer something they perceive as valuable.

4. We need to follow up—to let visitors know that they're appreciated, to invite them to other activities they might find appealing, to give them more opportunities to meet Christians who share their interests and concerns, and to draw them closer to the regular ministry of the church.

5. We need to incorporate regular visitors and new members into

our ministries as soon as possible. In this way, they will be able to see and participate in Christianity in action rather than just hear about it.

Urban churches beckon. We need people—and we need to *be* people—with the faith to persevere, the heart to love, the vision to see beyond the pollution and crowds and armor plating to vulnerable hearts seeking other hearts, and ultimately, the heart of Christ.

We need to catch God's vision of the city and its people. As Rebecca Pippert said, "When we go out into the world we ought never forget that we are interacting with potential royalty. We might be conversing with an heir apparent."[10] C. S. Lewis said the same thing:

> It is a serious thing to live in a society of possible gods and goddesses, to remember that the dullest and most uninteresting person you talk to may one day be a creature which if you saw it now, you would be strongly tempted to worship or else a horror and a corruption such as you now meet, if at all, only in a nightmare....There are no *ordinary* people. You have never met a mere mortal....But it is immortals we joke with, work with, marry, snub, and exploit—immortal horrors or everlasting splendors.[11]

God's vision for the city is that each of us as his people do what we can to help those around us to realize their potential for immortality and splendor. Our task is to see the city and its people as God sees them, as he sees us, and to build bridges connecting us as God's people with the city around us.

Questions for Discussion

1. Discuss the congregations you've been a part of and the ways you've served in them.

2. What are some strategies that might get your congregation better known in its neighborhood?

3. What are some of the strengths of your congregation that would be attractive to people around you?

4. Considering the three rings of Biblical text, faith community and urban context, which is your congregation strong in? How can you strengthen an area that's weak?

5. Brainstorm some ways that you can build bridges to your community.

CHAPTER 7

Being Like Jesus

Fiesta La Ballona is an annual community fair held at Veteran's Park in Culver City. There's a petting zoo and rides for the smaller children. Members of the Boy Scouts and the Rotary Club cook hamburgers and hot dogs, women from the Senior Center sell baked goods, ethnic organizations serve everything from Native American flatbread to Mexican, Persian and Thai food. For a nominal fee, church members were able to rent a booth, design a game for the children, and talk with their parents while the children played—handing out brochures and flyers about the church and its activities. For many years Fiesta was held in May—a perfect time to tell parents about VBS in the summer.

Keith Brisco was the deacon in charge of Fiesta. Keith sells plastics on the international market, but more than being a salesman, Keith loves people. He especially loves children, and he and his wife have done an excellent job of rearing their own two.

Keith took his ministry seriously, working with artists and carpenters to design the best games possible for the kids to play and constantly looking out for good prizes. At first, I bought big bags of cheap plastic animals, bugs and jewelry to have something to give the winners. Keith was embarrassed by my paltry prizes. He wanted to give the kids something better.

But the best thing Keith gave the children was himself. We had children who came back to our booth every year, often again and again over the two days of Fiesta, because of Keith. He always remembered their names. He always took the time to listen. He was quick to reassure those with poor coordination that "those were just practice shots. The real game starts now."

No one can bring smiles to sad faces like Keith can. When people look at Keith, they see love, concern, compassion and grace. When people look at Keith, they see Jesus. That's what we as God's children in the city are here for, isn't it? As Philip Yancey said in *The Jesus I Never Knew*, "The church serves as an extension of the Incarnation, God's primary way of establishing presence in the world."[1]

Earlier, Yancey had written:

> Three temples appear in the Bible, and, taken together, they illustrate a progression; God revealed himself first as Father, then as Son, and finally as Holy Spirit. The first temple was a magnificent structure built by Solomon and rebuilt by Herod. The second was the "temple" of Jesus' body ("Destroy it," he said, "and I will raise it again in three days"). And now a third temple has taken shape, fashioned out of individual human beings.[2]

God's third temple is the church, us, his people. Christ came to earth to share with us. He was incarnated, took on our fleshly nature so we might take on his spiritual nature. He took on our sin so we could share his perfection. He reconciled us to God. Because of Christ, God doesn't see us as sinful people any more. He sees us as having been washed, cleansed by Christ's sacrifice. When he looks at us, he sees Jesus.

> The doctrine of the Holy Spirit is the doctrine of "the church": God living in us. Such a plan is the "foolishness of God," as Paul says in one place, and writer Frederick Buechner marvels at the folly: "to choose for his holy work in the world…lamebrains and misfits and nickpickers and holier-than-thous and stuffed shirts and odd ducks and egomaniacs and milquetoasts and closet sensualists."[3]

In other words, God chose *us* to do his work in the world. We represent him. We are Jesus in action today. We see it again in the collection taken by Paul for the poor saints in Jerusalem:

When a famine broke out in Jerusalem, Paul himself led a fund-raising effort among all the churches he had founded. God was meeting the needs of the young church as surely as he had met the needs of the Israelites, but he was doing so indirectly, through fellow members of his body. Paul made no such distinction as "the church did this, but God did that." Such a division would miss the point he had made so often. The church is Christ's body; therefore if the church did it, God did it.[4]

When God looks at us, he sees Jesus. It isn't God's eyes that have changed. We have changed. We are no longer the same people. And we no longer see other people the same way either. We see them as potential saints, washed in Christ's blood, redeemed by his sacrifice and reconciled to God. Yancey concludes,

> My friend Richard had asked, "Where is God? Show me. I want to see him." Surely at least part of the answer to his question is this: If you want to see God, then look at the people who belong to him—they are his "bodies." They are the body of Christ.[5]

This principle of sharing, of incarnation, extends beyond Jesus and us to all people everywhere. Jesus wants everyone to share what we've experienced. And he wants us to initiate the process, just as he did when he came to earth. He took on our flesh and shared our experience. He wants us to put him on, to become himself incarnate in the world, to share him with those around us. How do we do that?

We incarnate Jesus by touching others with his grace

The gospel is more than just something to be taught. It is something to be lived. As Leighton Ford points out,

> You offer the touch of God's grace whenever you lend your presence and your practical, helping touch to people with a hurt or need. . . . Our touch cannot tell the story; only our voice can do that. But the touch of grace makes the story of grace come alive.[6]

The loving, sacrificial quality of our lives can say more about the Jesus we serve than hours of testimony. As Lewis Drummond says,

"Social action is vital to ministry....In the high hours of the church, God's covenant people have risen to meet the social needs of the world as well as to meet its spiritual poverty."[7]

How do we as Christ's church incarnate Christ in our community?

We incarnate Jesus by serving him

It may seem harder to serve Jesus today, in the time between his first and second comings. It may seem that he's gone away and left us on our own. But he hasn't. Jesus is all around us in the city, Yancey says. It's just that he's "taken on a disguise, a most unlikely disguise of the stranger, the poor, the hungry, the prisoner, the sick, the ragged ones of earth."[8]

Yancey bases this remarkable statement on the parable of the sheep and the goats (Matthew 25:31-46), the picture of the judgment scene where Jesus equates serving him with serving the rejected and the needy.

> According to this parable, Jesus knew that the world he left behind would include the poor, the hungry, the prisoners, the sick. The decrepit state of the world did not surprise him. He made plans to cope with it: a long-range plan and a short-range plan. The long-range plan involves his return, in power and great glory, to straighten out planet earth. The short-range plan means turning it over to the ones who will ultimately usher in the liberation of the cosmos. He ascended so that we would take his place.
>
> "Where is God when it hurts?" I have often asked. The answer is another question, "Where is the church when it hurts?"[9]

It's a staggering thought. God has turned the world over to us. That may be one sense of the phrase, "the body of Christ." Since Jesus ascended into heaven and his physical body no longer walks among us, we are now his body—*his* eyes that look with compassion on a needy world, *his* ears that hear its cries, *his* mouth that speaks comfort and hope, *his* hands that minister—touching the afflicted, binding wounds, handing out cups of cold water.

Yancey continues his musings in a vein that convicts all of us. "Why don't we look more like the church Jesus described? Why does the body of Christ so faintly resemble him?...I cannot provide a confident answer to such questions, for I am part of the problem. Examined closely, my query takes on a distressingly personal cast. Why do I so poorly resemble him?"[10]

How do we come better to resemble Jesus? How do we become churches that relate to the city, that open our arms to those who need our love and care?

We incarnate Jesus by meeting needs

When I first moved into the Culver City area, I was warned not to bother trying to work with the schools, because the Jewish people who were deeply involved in them insisted on keeping Christians out. I was determined not to let what other people said discourage me from reaching out to our community in any way I could. I began networking with the local schools and soon discovered that Jewish people are active in the schools because they care deeply about children. Because many had Christian beliefs and practices forced on them when they were children without regard for their beliefs, they insist on the clause in the Constitution that prohibits the establishment of religion. We can't teach Christ or evangelize in the schools. But they are willing—even eager—to work with anyone who has the children's best interests at heart.

Our benevolence programs are greatly appreciated by the local schools. Culver City is a changing community. Though most of the area is middle class, there are pockets of real need—particularly among the children of single mothers.

The one activity, more than any other, that has helped us develop relationships with local schools is our annual School Store, modeled on the ministry of the Highland Church of Christ in Memphis, Tennessee. Their minister, Harold Shank, impressed me years earlier with his innovative and needed services to his community. When I came to Culver Palms, I talked with him frequently about strategies for community outreach.

Harold taught me two tests of outreach: First, you have to provide a service that is needed. Second, you have to let people know about it. By mixing benevolence and publicity, the church both serves the needy and raises its profile among community people who appreciate what we're doing. As Jesus put it in the Sermon on the Mount, "Let your light so shine before people, that they may see your good works and glorify your Father in heaven" (Matthew 5:16).

We incarnate Jesus by linking ministries

We didn't want just to hand people something and then forget about them, no matter how much they needed what we had to offer. I began looking for ways to increase our contact with the families that came to School Store. A call from the office of our State Assemblyman Kevin Murray opened one way for us. Kevin's deputy asked if we would be willing to distribute turkeys to fifty families at Thanksgiving.

We took the project a step further, holding a food drive and raising funds to pack fifty bags of groceries to go with the turkeys. Then we called the families that had participated in School Store and invited them back to pick up a complete Thanksgiving dinner, together with rice and beans to stretch it out for a week.

We incarnate Jesus by giving God room to work

Bernard L. Ramm, in his book *His Way Out: A Fresh Look at Exodus*, writes,

> God works in the pushes and pulls of history even though we who live in the midst of history and cannot see the end from the beginning have no way of detecting his work. But faith believes he is there: In Egypt! at the cross! in our lives! in our history of our world in our times![11]

And sometimes, we see him working. In December, we invited the School Store children back for our Angel Tree Party. We had written the names and ages of the children from our School Store list on paper angels and hung them on a Christmas tree. Members of the church took the angels and purchased gifts for the children whose names were on them. Then the singles and the teens helped give a party for them, complete with games, cookies to decorate, a puppet show, and a visit from Santa.

One year my daughter, Kathy, who was a member of the singles group, took an angel from the tree that read, "Juan, 16." Juan was older than most of the Angel Tree kids, so she asked some of the teens to help her think of a gift he might like. They suggested a Walkman, and she bought it, wrapped it and put it under the tree.

She was helping give the party that year, and when Juan's name was called, she was surprised to see a tall, gangly youth walk slowly to the front and plop down on Santa's lap. His feet touched the floor. Juan was developmentally disabled.

When Santa asked Juan what he wanted for Christmas, he said a Walkman, and when he opened his present, his smile was a mile wide. His parents fought back tears as they told us how much he had wanted the gift they couldn't afford to buy.

"Was that set up?" the deacon playing Santa asked after the party. "Did his parents tell you what he wanted in advance?"

They didn't. We may strategize for outreach, but God makes the miracles!

We incarnate Jesus by empowering people to help themselves

About the time I left the Vermont Avenue Church for Culver Palms, talk had begun about welfare reform—requiring people to get off welfare and into jobs. It sounded good in theory, but I was concerned about what would happen when a flood of untrained and inexperienced people entered the sophisticated Los Angeles job market. How could they compete? Would they end up in minimum wage, temporary positions that didn't pay enough to support their families or offer any real hope?

The children of single mothers are among the poorest residents of Los Angeles County. How would they survive if their mothers couldn't get decent jobs? I was afraid that welfare reform would only exacerbate problems like poverty and homelessness.

Work is basic to human life. God made people, placed them in a garden, and gave them work to do (Genesis 2:15). According to the Oxford Declaration,

> Since work is central to God's purpose for humanity, people everywhere have both the obligation and the right to work....The right to work...should be understood as part of the freedom of the individual to contribute to the satisfaction of the needs of the community. It is a...form of self-expression."[12]

And Ronald Sider wrote, "God wants all people to have the productive resources to earn a decent living and be dignified members of their community."[13]

By that time, I was working with a church that had the capacity to make a difference. Unlike the aging and dwindling membership at

Vermont Avenue, the Culver Palms Church was a larger, younger, more affluent group of people. The elders had hired me to do community outreach, and I asked interested members to join me on an outreach committee to determine the direction that ministry should take.

Others shared my concerns about welfare reform, so the committee decided to look into offering a job training program.

We examine the need

According to the 1990 census, there was great economic disparity among families in our area. With Mar Vista Gardens housing project on one side of us and Beverly Hills on the other, the extremes were obvious. Whereas a married couple with children had a mean income of $67,319, a female householder with children had a mean income of $25,967. The per capita income of Latino households was only half that of whites. Single Latino mothers would be hardest hit by proposed cuts in government assistance.

Bruce Rankin, director of the Westside Food Bank, estimated that the first cuts in federal welfare programs would leave some 12,000 people on the Westside hungry, rising to many times that number once cuts in Aid to Families with Dependent Children (AFDC) kicked in.

Culver City was in the midst of a downtown revitalization effort with funding for business owners to upgrade their storefronts, parking incentives for restaurants, outdoor dining, wider sidewalks, new trees, plants and benches. According to the International and Public Affairs Center at Occidental College, this is one of two ways to do community redevelopment:

> Development strategies in low-income neighborhoods have tended to be either "place-based" or "people-based." Place-based programs focus on improving an area in hopes of attracting business, building community and retaining economically successful residents....People-based strategies focus more on building up individual human capital or skills, connecting low-income residents to jobs wherever they may be.[14]

While the city was pursuing one strategy, we felt called to pursue the other. Jesus, in his interaction with the lawyer (Luke 10:25-37), says we are to love our neighbor as ourselves. When the lawyer asks, "Who is my neighbor?" Jesus answers by telling him how to *be* a neighbor—by showing mercy to those who have been damaged by life. Then he told him to "go and do likewise." As God's children in the city charged with loving our neighbors as ourselves, our primary focus is on people, not places. We decided to follow the Samaritan's example by investing money, time and effort in being neighbors to those in our community who had been left out of the job market and battered by circumstances.

We design a program

As we considered how to prepare single mothers in our area to get jobs, we decided to see what churches in other parts of the country were doing. Ruth Johnson, a former community college president and higher education professor at Pepperdine, agreed to help. In November of 1996, Ruth and I attended the Urban Ministries Conference in Dallas. While we were there, we toured the facilities of Central Dallas Ministries. They had a food pantry, medical and dental programs, and job training. Job training was the part that caught our attention.

While we were at the conference, we met with a group from Memphis Area Community Services (MACS), which offers the Adkins Life Skills Lab job preparation curriculum developed at Columbia University. Used by municipalities and Head Starts across the country, as well as by the Los Angeles Urban League, the Adkins curriculum is known for the excellent job retention rate of its graduates. Of twenty-two graduates of the Memphis program by April 1992, ninety percent had begun some work or training opportunity. Seventy percent remained in work or school for over six months.[15]

Adkins trains students to identify their abilities, interests and values; obtain and interpret occupational information; make realistic and informed career decisions, master job-seeking skills; use personal and professional contacts; manage time effectively; set short- and long-term goals; complete application forms, prepare resumes and write cover letters; develop effective interviewing skills; and formulate strategies to keep a job. The curriculum includes audio- and videotapes, teacher's and students' guides, and activities for each of the ten weeks of the program.

Ruth reviewed curricula from across the nation and decided on the Adkins program. With a combined emphasis on serving people and changing lives, we felt the longer Adkins format was perfect for us.

Students would attend class from 9 a.m. until 2 p.m. Monday through Friday for ten weeks. That allowed parents to drop off their children at school before coming to study with us, then pick them up after.

It allowed us to compensate in depth for what we couldn't offer in size or speed. Our program would be comprehensive, would provide a strong support network, and would prepare students for starting salaries of at least eight dollars an hour (at a time when minimum wage was $5.75), with opportunities for advancement. It would take at least that much to support families of two or three children.

The elders agreed to pay the costs of the curriculum and of training teachers to use it. To better serve the entire person, we supplemented the basic Adkins curriculum with daily devotions and journaling. Computer training in word processing and spreadsheets in a Windows environment added a marketable skill.

Support services were designed to remove obstacles that might prevent students from successfully completing the course. Each student was assigned a mentor from the congregation. Child care referrals, bus tokens and the church's food pantry were made available. The Back-to-Work Boutique provided good used clothing suitable for interviews. Life Skills Lab students and their families would be included in the regular benevolence ministries of the Culver Palms Church, including School Store, the Thanksgiving turkey distribution, and the Angel Tree Christmas party.

We offer classes

A pilot class of seven students began meeting in September of 1997. Ruth was the classroom teacher, and I directed the program. All of the students were minority women with children. Most were single mothers.

Maria[16] wasn't. Maria called us before the program began. Her children attended La Ballona Elementary School, the school nearest our building. The families of students there are the poorest in the Culver City School District.

Maria had been a school teacher in her native Chile. Here she cleaned people's houses, and her husband was a janitor. They had three children. She cried as she talked about working all day with nobody to talk with. "I'm forgetting all my English," she said. "I feel worthless."

I knew we could help with her English skills and self-esteem, but there was another serious consideration. "If I come to your class, I'll have to quit my job," she explained. "Will I make more money if I do?" "We can't make any promises," I said. "But we will do our best to prepare you for a better job than housekeeping."

Several days later, she called back. She and her husband had talked long and hard and decided to give it a try. She quit her job and came to study at Life Skills Lab.

Maria and six other students did more than just form the first class of Life Skills Lab. They gave all of us—both those who worked directly with the program and those who didn't—a chance to be like Jesus, to let our light shine before seven community people who were meeting daily at our building.

We incarnate Jesus in daily living

What does it mean to be like Jesus? That was the first question we asked ourselves. Many of us had studied about Jesus all our lives. Now we were faced with the question of how to translate that "head knowledge" into daily living. How did he live as a person on earth? What was he like? What did he do?[17]

He wasn't what you'd expect—the Savior of the world in the form of a helpless baby lying on a bed of hay. Going from being with his father in glory to being poor, helpless and lowly here on earth. Paul says of Jesus that, though he was rich, he became poor for our sakes (2 Corinthians 8:9). It was a choice he made, a gift of grace to us.

J. I. Packer, in *Knowing God*, speaks of

> what it meant for the Son of God to empty himself and become poor. It meant a laying aside of glory; a voluntary restraint of power; an acceptance of hardship, isolation, ill-treatment, malice and misunderstanding; finally, a death that involved such agony—spiritual even more than physical—that his mind nearly broke under the prospect of it....At the Father's will Jesus Christ became poor and was born in a stable so that thirty years later he might hang on a cross. It is the most wonderful message that the world has ever heard or will hear.[18]

The Book of Luke was written to proclaim God's justice to outcasts and poor people. Time and again, it emphasizes Jesus' concern for the poor and despised, expressed both in example and in teaching. As he began his ministry, Jesus returned to his hometown of Nazareth and read from Isaiah 61:1-2 in the synagogue (See Luke 4:16-22):

> The Spirit of the Lord is upon Me,
> Because He has anointed Me
> To preach the gospel to the poor;
> He has sent Me to heal the brokenhearted,
> To proclaim liberty to those who are oppressed;
> To proclaim the acceptable year of the Lord.

This reading astonished the people who heard him, as it does us today. *They* were appalled that Jesus applied Messianic prophecy to himself. *We* are amazed that he identified with the poor and weak and despised. From his birth in a stable to his burial in a borrowed tomb, he turned our values upside down, showing us that worth is not measured by our standards of wealth and fame.

Three more times in the book of Luke, Jesus speaks of his purpose in coming to earth:

- In Luke 5:32, he says, "I have not come to call the righteous, but sinners, to repentance." Do we even know non-Christians, nevertheless bring them to Christ?
- In Luke 19:10, Jesus says that "the Son of Man has come to seek and to save that which was lost." Do we spend time working with lost and troubled people?
- Finally, in Luke 22:27, Jesus says, "I am among you as One who serves." Are we known for our lives of service?

How do you live like Jesus?

1. Find ways to be with people who aren't brothers and sisters in Christ. Get out in the community.
2. Touch people with God's grace. Do something to help others.
3. Discover a need in the community, and do what you can to meet it. Work as an individual, part of an established group, or part of a Christian ministry.
4. Encourage your congregation to get more involved, either as individuals or as a group.

5. Create relationships. Don't just hand out something and go on. Find ways to "keep in touch" with the recipients of your concern.
6. Give God room to work. Pray in expectation that God will take your efforts and make something special from them.
7. Look for ways to empower the people you help to help themselves.

As Christians, we're called to be like Jesus—to live Christlike lives in our cities today, continuing his pattern of "turning the world upside down." It's a call, Packer says, to reproduce "in human lives...the temper of him who for our sakes became poor."

But, he concedes, we don't always hear or respond to that call.

So many of the soundest and most orthodox Christians go through this world in the spirit of the priest and the Levite in our Lord's parable, seeing human needs all around them, but (after a pious wish, and perhaps a prayer, that God might meet those needs) averting their eyes and passing by on the other side.

What a contrast with "the spirit of those who, like their master, live their whole lives on the principle of making themselves poor—spending and being spent—to enrich their fellow humans, giving time, trouble, care and concern, to do good to others...in whatever way there seems need."[19]

Our God still does the unexpected. He still uses the unlikely and sends the extraordinary. And he still proclaims a revolutionary message, still turns things upside down! As his people, we want to be found working with him—crying and praying for our city, meeting its needs, touching its people with God's grace, reaching out to the poor and lost with a gospel of hope—seeing our city with the eyes of God!

Questions for Discussion

1. How was Jesus incarnated as a person on earth 2,000 years ago?

2. How can Jesus be incarnated in our cities today?

3. How can you "link" ministries in your congregation—using a contact list from one activity to inform visitors about another activity they might enjoy or benefit from to continue contact with the same people?

4. What is a basic need in your community that the church can address?

5. What does it mean to be like Jesus?

CHAPTER 8

Wonders in Our Paths

As I walked into Veteran's Auditorium, I was confronted with a sea of tables. I stopped and prayed, but had absolutely no sense of where to go. I stood for a while and prayed again. Still no direction. I turned and walked back up the aisle, and two men talking near the door stopped and opened it for me. I introduced myself and gave them my card, telling them about our new Life Skills Lab. They were officers of the Exchange Club, a local civic organization, and they invited me to speak at their next meeting.

At that meeting, I was nervous and flustered and nothing seemed to come out right, but one club member, Ron Arsenault, literally followed me around the buffet table. He had a lot of questions and offered to help us get computers. I invited him to meet with our community service committee. He came to the next meeting, which was held just before evening service. He began worshipping with us, first on Sunday evenings after the meetings, then on Sunday mornings. He was baptized a few months later and still is active in the church.

Networking is effective. Networking with prayer is dynamite!

In the busy months leading up to our first Life Skills Lab class, I felt a growing need to stay close to God and trust him for wisdom and strength. I prayed daily and kept a journal of those prayers and devotional thoughts, as well as practical concerns that arose.

Limited as it was, Life Skills Lab was too ambitious for just one 350-member church. I had started networking in the community when I was hired to do community outreach, joining the Chamber of Commerce and working with the local schools. Now, with greater needs facing us, I prayed to make the contacts we needed. Suddenly, I was inundated with invitations.

At a meeting of the Chamber of Commerce education committee, a woman sat down beside me and introduced herself as Joan Jakubowski. Joan was the president of the School Board. She became a member of our Advisory Board and a valued friend. She called me "the angel from the Church of Christ." One day, she told me that we were doing "what churches are supposed to do." That was the view of many in our community, both those who needed our services and those who, like Ron and Joan, were in a position to help.

I joined the Healthy Start Collaborative at La Ballona School, became part of a task force to identify needy families in the Culver City School District, and joined a group organizing the local Service Planning Area of the County Children's Planning Council to improve delivery of county services. Connections with these groups would lead to new students for the program, new supporters from the community, and contact with potential funding sources.

I attended the organizing meeting for the American Heart Association, where the director of Early Childhood Education for the school district offered free child care for our students with preschool children. I also attended a seminar on Building Livable Communities on the Westside. Before each meeting I'd ask God to lead me to the person I was there to meet—the person who could help us with our program.

Prayer powers ministry

Prayer is the fuel that powers ministry. Prayer is the means by which we reach beyond ourselves and our own resources to tap into the power of the Creator of the universe. However, as J. I. Packer says,

> To many people, guidance is a chronic problem. Why? Not because they doubt that divine guidance is a fact, but because they are sure it is. They know that God can guide, and has promised to guide, every Christian believer. Books and friends

and public speakers tell them how guidance has worked in the lives of others. Their fear, therefore, is not that no guidance should be available for them, but that they may miss the guidance which God provides through some fault of their own.

* * * * *

Belief that divine guidance is real rests upon two foundation-facts: first, the reality of God's plan for us; second, the ability of God to communicate with us.[1]

Packer points out that "God has a plan for each of his children" and that he "has no difficulty in making his will known to his servants." He continues that "*Wisdom* in scripture always means knowledge of the course of action that will please God and secure life, so that the promise of James 1:5—"If any of you lacks wisdom, let him ask God, who gives to all men generously and without reproaching, and it will be given him'— is in effect a promise of guidance."[2]

All too often, however, my prayers have gone from seeking to please God and discern his will to communicating my desires to him and seeking his buy-in on a project or direction I've already determined. According to Robert Kolb,

> Prayer does not provide the all-knowing God with information which he previously did not have at his disposal. It provides instead the opportunity for God to enjoy conversation with his children, who cannot resist chatting with him and sharing their needs and joys. Prayer does not offer some special power to those who pray; prayer has no power of its own, such as that of a pagan magical incantation designed to put a hammerlock on God. Prayer rather offers the opportunity for God's children to express their aches and sorrows, their delights and hopes to their loving and beloved Father, confident that he alone exercises the power needed to deal properly with their concerns.[3]

We pray that God's will be done, not that our will be God's. When we confuse seeking God's guidance with seeking our own desires, we're on the road to disappointment. Only God can "deal properly with [our] concerns."

Nehemiah, an Urban Builder

The Old Testament character of Nehemiah (Nehemiah 1-13) was a particular inspiration to me at the time. Nehemiah had a big job to do, and he often turned to God for the strength and resources he needed to do it. Nehemiah was cupbearer to the king of Persia after the fall of Jerusalem. He was commissioned by the king to rebuild the walls of the city. In addition to being a governmental official involved in urban renewal,

Nehemiah was a man of prayer. He prayed over the need for stronger defenses for the city; he prayed for success in getting the funds to meet those needs; and he prayed for help to resist opposition to his efforts.

Nehemiah was well organized. He had a clear grasp of the material and human resources the project required.

Nehemiah was motivated. He continued the work despite opposition from without and oppression from within. He sacrificed personally to carry out his work.

Nehemiah was honest. He kept good accounts of the people and materials used in the project—accounts that remain even today.

Nehemiah was a spiritual leader. He encouraged the reading of the Word, led in worship and celebration, and led in confession of sins.

We pray for practical concerns

Taking my cue from Nehemiah, I asked God for everything we needed, large and small, spiritual and material. Through the month of August, we worked on getting computers donated, putting together an intake process, planning an open house for prospective students, learning about fundraising, getting volunteers to work as mentors, and finding volunteers to do business studies.

Business students from Pepperdine University did a needs analysis and a marketing plan as part of a service learning project. The needs analysis turned up more demand for our classes than we could possibly meet. Of twelve local service agencies surveyed, eight indicated that they could refer a total of 61-72 students.[4]

Two local schools surveyed almost 200 parents and discovered that 64 wanted work but couldn't find jobs, 93 worked but would be interested in training for a new job, and 40 were "particularly interested in job training."[5] The Healthy Start program in these and other local schools referred parents of their students for training.

We pray for revival

As important as it was to get to know people who could work with us and to get help with our physical needs, it was even more important to pray for our spiritual needs, both as individuals and as a body of God's people. It is a temptation, especially in a congregation of gifted professionals like Culver Palms, to fall into a pattern of self-reliance and fail to recognize and acknowledge our dependence on God. Thankfully, the Culver Palms Church has always been a praying church, especially dedicated to praying for the physical health of its members and praising God when those prayers are answered. All that was needed was to extend those prayers to include people outside our walls. I felt we were ready to take that step.

On June 26, I prayed, "Heavenly Father, I sense a growing urgency and reliance on you. I pray that you'll sweep our churches of self-reliance and make us all depend on you to reach our potential for service. Grant us a revival as we work among the people of this area. Help us begin really to grow at Culver—to retain the people we bring in. Lord, we need you, and we need your direction to do your work. Help us discover what you would have us do. I'm still amazed at the wonders you scatter in our paths. Help us recognize and appreciate and take advantage of them. Lord, make me open to all the possibilities."[6]

Even when the way seemed unclear or things looked hopeless, I tried to remember to pray and not worry. On June 28 I prayed, "Heavenly Father, Thank you for loving us enough to send Jesus, for loving us enough that your will is always for our good. Thank you for knowing so completely, that you know what's best for us even when we can't see how it can work. And thank you for having the power to work out circumstances in front of us so your will can be done."

I felt that God wanted the congregation to stretch itself even more than it was. "I believe that it is your will that Culver Palms use some of its vast resources of material goods and talents to glorify you by serving others."

We commit our plans to God

In May, Larry James preached for us and talked about Dallas Urban Ministries. After worship, members of the community outreach committee had lunch with him at a local restaurant to discuss our plans for Life Skills Lab.

The next week, we held an Open Forum on Sunday evening. The committee presented plans and answered questions about the ministry for members of our congregation and visitors from neighboring ones, including the Hollywood church, Malibu, and Hawthorne.

The next week was Fiesta La Ballona, the Culver City community festival at Veteran's Park. We handed out information about Life Skills Lab at our booth there.

In June, we planned a "No to Violence" event to present Life Skills Lab to the broader community. Two members of our artists' group, Desiree and Cuauhtemoc Arrieta, designed posters and flyers on the theme, "Off the Streets and into Jobs: Fighting Violence with Job Training." News releases and press kits were prepared, and nearby congregations were invited.

As time for No to Violence drew near, I prayed, "We're getting these flyers done, and we need to get them out to all the people who need to come and hear about our program. You know who those people are. You already have our first class picked out. Whoever they are, help us receive them warmly and work with them creatively. Help us find mentors who will provide that personal touch of love and concern."

We prepared registration sheets for No to Violence and application forms for the Life Skills Lab class. Volunteers were assigned for set-up, parking, child care, and clean up. As the number of people giving their time, talents and money grew, I prayed, "Help all of us—all the people you've brought together for Life Skills Lab, and all those you'll be bringing together. Help us and bless us to do your will. Use us to make an impact beyond our financial resources, beyond our time and energy resources. Take care of us and keep us and work through us to bring many to you."

We pray for strength and persistence

It was a busy summer. The No to Violence meeting to launch Life Skills Lab was just one of a number of congregational activities. As a staff member, I was involved in many of them. As the day of the meeting approached, the demands seemed to be outstripping my resources. On July 8, I wrote, "Heavenly Father, thank you that you want a relationship with me as an individual. Thank you that you make your will known in various ways. Thank you especially for your Word. I've always read it as a general message to all your people, which it is. But if you have a message for me personally, help me be alert to it. Right now, it seems to be perseverance, continuing faithful. I am getting tired. Give me the strength I need."

As much as I was able, I tried to release the project to God. "Father, these efforts are our gifts to you. They are crude and poorly done, but please take them and make of them something to glorify you. Help our neighbors to know that you are, that you love and care, that you live in us and want to live in them."

A week before No to Violence, everything seemed to be falling apart. Several people didn't follow through with responsibilities they said they'd handle, our minister was sick, a much-loved former elder died, there was dissension in the congregation over the role of women in worship, and the contribution was down. I prayed that those concerns wouldn't distract us from the opportunity that lay before us. "Father, I'm really concerned and harried, and I'm a little overwhelmed with all that needs doing. Please help me and strengthen me. Show me how to look at what's happening in my life and in the life of the church. I pray that it isn't something we can't recover from. We need you, Lord. Bless us with your presence. Father, show me your will in this situation. How can you be glorified through it all? Help me find ways to glorify you as I live through this confusion."

We pray for faith and vision

The summer before Life Skills Lab began, I attended a care group that was studying Henry Blackaby's *Experiencing God.* The Blackaby study encouraged me to try to see all that was happening through God's eyes.[7] On July 13, I prayed, "Heavenly Father, Thank you for loving us and caring for us to this day. We are taking on a task too big for us, one that only you can accomplish. I believe you want us to do this work. I believe you are calling us to do this work. I believe you will enable us to do this work. We will proceed in faith, and we will watch to see your provision. You already have littered my path with such wonderful surprises. I've seen them, but most people haven't. Now I'm asking you to do something so big that nobody can miss it. Do a work we can't do, one only you can do."

Turning it over to God

On July 17, the morning of No to Violence, I prayed that God would bless our efforts. "Heavenly Father, We've done our work. Now we rely on you, as we have through the entire process. Please bring people to us tonight. Help us reach those people we need to reach—who can be students, employers, and supporters of our efforts."

I picked up Harold Shank, our speaker, at the airport and took him to lunch with our minister, the elders, Ruth Johnson, the Life Skills Lab teacher, and Marvin Cooper, assistant teacher. After lunch, Harold came home with me, and we discussed the challenges facing us. I was concerned about how seriously people would take me as a woman in ministry. Harold encouraged me to do my best and trust God.

The meeting that night was inspiring. Dean Shaw, a deacon and member of the community outreach committee, served as emcee. Ruth and Marvin, together with Gloria Crawford Vitulo, a public school teacher on the committee, formed a panel to discuss the educational principles behind the program. Harold told inspiring stories about the changes Life Skills Lab had made in the lives of some of those in the classes in Memphis. Among those attending were agency leaders from the community, the local fire chief, and a personnel manager from TRW.

We pray for the varied aspects of the classes

No to Violence was just the prelude to the classes scheduled to begin in September, but it made me more aware than ever of the responsibility that was ours as the various parts of the church and community were coming together to meet the students' needs. "Lord, bless the people who come to us," I prayed. "May those who need training and encouragement find it. May those who need better employees see this as one source. May the student volunteers who come from Pepperdine be inspired for urban ministry. Bless all who come needing to believe in you, whether they realize it or not. Help them find you here. Help all of us grow in faith as we see your wonders performed among us here in Los Angeles. Father, I know you have the power and wisdom and love to use us to do great things for you and for the people around us. May you be glorified."

Even before the program began, I realized that it would be easy to lose focus among the myriad demands of a program like Life Skills Lab.

I prayed, "Lord, we need your help and strength and guidance in these and all our efforts for you. Help us to keep perspective and realize that it isn't the projects that are important but the people being helped, the people doing the helping and that your name is glorified. Glorify your name here in Los Angeles through us, your people."

Testing was held on September 9. "Bless our testing today," I prayed. "Be with everyone who comes for it. Help us get just the people we need to have a really good class. Be with Ruth and Judye (our computer lab teacher) and Marvin as they prepare to teach. Bless our mentors and the support ministries. Bless the Culver Palms Church to see the worth of our efforts and be glad for their part in helping." God answered our prayers as 13 church members volunteered to serve as mentors for the seven students who had signed up to take the classes. We were able to choose the best mentor for each individual student.

The day before the first class began, I asked God to help us have good attitudes. "We're embarking on a daunting project Monday morning. Bless us and bless the students through us. Help us give them things that are nothing but helpful. Father God, we need you. Give us an extra portion of your Spirit so we can be kind and patient, but know when it will be more helpful to be tough."

We see God's hand

The next day, class began with six students. Ruth taught the class with Marvin assisting. Judye taught the computer lab. We soon learned the truth of the statement by Muhammed Yunus, founder of the Grameen Bank in India, that "poor women have the intense drive to move up, they are hard working, concerned about their human dignity, concerned about their children's present and future, willing to make personal sacrifices for the well-being of their children."[8] We had done well to concentrate on single mothers, both from the standpoint of need and of motivation.

Through the participatory, team-building techniques that are a part of the Adkins curriculum, the students became a peer support group. Their ties only strengthened as they prayed for each other and discussed their progress.

God was with us, and everything seemed to come together wonderfully. I prayed, "Lord, we can't do it without you. You know even better than I do how much you've intervened and touched people and worked events to bring us to this point. Continue to keep and guard us. Thank you more than I can say for the wonderful way you've blessed us until now."

We seek God's help with technology

One of our problems was with computers. The limited number of computers that were donated for the first class, together with the space constraints of holding classes in the church building, meant that we had to set up the computers before computer lab on Monday and take them down and store them in a closet over the weekend. That was hard on both personnel and equipment. At one point, breakdowns left us with just two working computers for the class.

Individuals were kind to donate computers, but it soon became apparent that, by the time they were ready to give them up, the computers had very little life left. It was a challenge to the abilities of our hardware expert, Pride Joseph. I prayed, "Heavenly Father, thank you so much that we are going to have computers Friday. Please help us continue working on the problem, and provide us with a more permanent and consistent solution."

Our prayers were answered at our benefit brunch that year when one of our deacons announced that his company, Bank of America, was donating ten reconditioned computers to Life Skills Lab.

We pray for student needs

Serving students through Life Skills Lab wasn't confined to offering training. The women who came to us had problems, and it took a continuous effort to help them address those problems and remain in class.

Louisa's daughter threw her out of her house because she didn't want her studying with us. I got her into temporary housing provided by the local Catholic church, and when that was up, I brought her home to stay with Frank and me until she was able to patch things up with her daughter.

When Teresa started training, her unemployment check stopped coming. A single mother with three children, she needed that money. I tried several ways of dealing with the problem, calling the constantly busy number of the EDD (Employment Development Department) and asking to speak to a supervisor at each level when I was told there was nothing they could do. I wondered if it was time to call on Kevin Murray, the state assemblyman who provided turkeys for our Thanksgiving food distribution. "Be with me at work today," I prayed. "Be with Teresa and let her unemployment be reinstated. Father, we need your help. If I should call Kevin's office, please let me know that. And if I should wait until we've done the paper work and seen what the EDD decides, let me know that. Lord, I'm frightened to be trying to intervene in people's lives this way. Show me my limits. Show me your will for my life. I've seen your hand in so much of our efforts for Life Skills Lab. Thank you for being with us and making it useful to these precious people."

Louisa eventually left the program and moved to Texas to live with other family members. We hated to lose her, but it may have been better for her in the long run. My prayer for Teresa, on the other hand, was answered with a powerful yes. The church loaned her the money to continue paying rent until her unemployment check was reinstated through the intervention of Kevin Murray. She repaid the loan promptly. And on October 6, we found out that our program had been okayed by the EDD. Future students would be spared the problems Teresa experienced.

I share the story

I was so excited about God's work through us and Life Skills Lab that I took advantage of every opportunity I was given to speak about it. The first weekend in October, I spoke for our women's retreat. Before the talk, I prayed, "Heavenly Father, help me capture the wonderful sense of what your people are capable of being, and help me communicate it clearly and forcefully. Help me share my experience with your guiding, especially in Life Skills Lab and my networking."

That year the World Missions Workshop, a gathering of college students from across the nation, was held at Pepperdine. The theme was urban ministry. I taught a class there, and a hundred college students from across the country came to Culver Palms to see our program.

"Help us find your direction for our work," I prayed. "Touch me again with your Spirit, Lord. Give me a new sense of vocation and commitment and love for you and the people around me. Bless us here at

Culver Palms as we look forward to tomorrow. Help us host the students who come to us in a way that makes them feel welcome, but more than that, that shows them some new ways of reaching out to the city."

We experience mountains and valleys

As usual, the mountaintop experience of the World Missions Workshop was followed by a valley of the mundane. I prayed, "Why, Lord, am I so covered over with work? Why can I never, ever get caught up? Why does each day bring more to cover up the work that was already piled up? What am I supposed to do to make it better? Lord, please give me a break—just a short break, and not one I have to get sick to get. Yet I know that, however busy I am, you are there. You can make sense of the confusion, and when you call me home to you, it will make no difference at all that I haven't caught up. My work will be finished."

By the next day, I was asking God to "help our students get good jobs. Bless those who are struggling. Thank you that, against all odds, Karen and Lupe seem to be thriving. Take care of them and of their health. Help them continue to flourish. Bless us all as we work together to lead these precious souls closer to you." Karen had an emotional problem and had been over-medicated. I suggested that she ask her doctor about reducing the dosage so she could be more alert in class. It worked! Lupe, a diabetic, was constantly eating junk food. We added a discussion of preventive medicine to the curriculum. God was answering our prayers and providing for our students' needs.

I seek perspective

A professional writer and editor who had been hired to do community outreach for a church, I was aware of my need for further training for the work I was now doing. Amy, a friend of a member of my writers' workshop, was attending Fuller Theological Seminary, and she suggested that I look into their urban ministry program. I called and was invited to Prospective Student Day.

Before I left that morning, I prayed, "Lord, I lift up this day before you....Guide me in deciding whether to attend Fuller. It would mean filling another evening, making another regular drive, studying—adding to my already full life. On the other hand, it would give me a little distance from my work, a chance to learn better how to do it, and the opportunity to share with people doing similar work." The day after Prospective Student Day, I decided to enroll.

There are some lessons you can't learn in a class. Some lessons have to be learned by experience—especially the lessons of our failure really to be God's people. A program like Life Skills Lab can make you look at yourself, and sometimes you don't like what you see. "We are to do justly, love mercy and walk humbly with you," I prayed. "I don't need to search the newspaper to discover that cutting people off welfare and telling them to get a job without training them is unjust and unmerciful. That's why we're working to redress the injustice—in just a few cases. Father, help us help, without trying to do everything. Motivate our students to do their part to make their lives better. If we truly work together, they can succeed, but we can't do it alone."

We celebrate success

On December 5, 1997, five women graduated from our pilot class at a potluck dinner held in the Fellowship Hall to celebrate their achievements. Six months later, Teresa had a full-time job at a bookstore. She started working nights to stock the shelves and progressed over time to be assistant to the owner—arranging window displays, ordering stock and keeping financial records.

Maria got a job working part-time for Venice Family Clinic, a free medical clinic. First she designed a child-care area at their facility, and when that was done, they hired her to explain the various free and low-cost health insurance programs to low-income families, especially those who spoke Spanish, and sign them up for the option they chose. Karen was studying to be a medical secretary, and Lupe was doing clerical work in an internship with ERAS Center, a school for children with developmental disabilities. The internship turned into a paid position.

Several of the students attended care groups, Bible studies and worship. Some continued the daily devotions they began in class. Teresa became a member of our advisory board. Maria spoke to later classes about the training she'd received at Life Skills Lab and signed up their children for free or low-cost health insurance. "We want to thank you for all you did for us by helping someone else," she said.

We learned a lot about working with people as Life Skills Lab began. We also learned a lot about prayer and trusting God. We learned

1. That God answers prayers.
2. That God cares about all aspects of our lives and ministries.
3. That we can depend on God.
4. That we have weaknesses that limit our effectiveness in ministry, and we need God's forgiveness.
5. That God supplies our needs—for people, material help, strength, knowledge, even technology.
6. That God is greater than the government and can intervene and change things.
7. That God always knows what's best.

When a child who asks for candy before dinner is told no, the mother hasn't failed to answer the request. She just hasn't answered the way the child wanted. In the same way, when God answers our prayers with a no, or even a wait, he hasn't failed to answer. It may be that he sees ramifications we can't see. God may say yes to one request and no to another, but he always answers, and we can trust him to give us what is best in the long run.

Heavenly Father, thank you for answering our prayers. Thank you for having the vision to see far beyond what we can see. Thank you for giving us an occasional glimpse of the possibilities as you see them for our lives and ministries. Fill us with your Spirit, and strengthen us to follow you—when we can see the way and when we can't. Teach us to trust and depend on you.

Questions for Discussion

1. How can you "network with prayer"?

2. How does prayer power ministry?

3. What are some big things you need God's guidance for? What are some smaller details you can ask him about?

4. How can you and your congregation learn to depend more on God?

5. What prayers have you seen answered in your ministries? Do they help you trust God more?

The Ministry

CHAPTER 9

Up Close and Personal

Jesus, in his interaction with the lawyer in Luke 10:25-37, identified the requirements of Christian living as loving God with all our heart, soul, mind and strength, and loving our neighbor as ourselves.

"And who is my neighbor?" the lawyer asked. It wasn't a question asked merely to gain information. Luke says that "he wanted to justify himself."

We can sympathize. We want to justify ourselves. We want to think that we're good Christian people without making any adjustments to our attitudes or behavior. But, in response to the man's question, Jesus told the Parable of the Good Samaritan.

In telling the parable, he didn't answer the lawyer's specific question, and he didn't allow the self-justification the lawyer sought. He didn't draw lines and say, "This person is your neighbor and you should love her, this one isn't, so you're exempt." Instead he told him how to *be* a neighbor—by showing mercy to those who have been damaged by life.

How did the Samaritan show mercy to the man he found beaten and battered by the side of the road?

1. *He treated the immediate problem.* Often the problem that is easiest to see—the need for food, shelter, or in this case, medical assistance—is not the major problem in a person's life. But it's a problem that has to be solved before you can get to the deeper needs. A student in one of our classes who lacked food or whose welfare check had

been cut would have trouble learning until that problem had been addressed.

2. *He removed the man from the dangerous environment.* The Samaritan didn't leave the injured man in the ditch. He took him to an inn where he could find safety and comfort. The environment of the Life Skills Lab classroom was a big change from what most of our students were accustomed to. Often they commented on how quiet it was. At first, some of them found it disconcerting, but later they grew to appreciate the chance to escape the stresses and distractions of their daily lives.

3. *He provided for the man's longer-term needs.* Not content just to bandage wounds and get the man out of the ditch, he provided for the man's care even after he had gone on. "The next day he took out two silver coins and gave them to the innkeeper. 'Look after him,' he said, 'and when I return, I will reimburse you for any extra expense you may have.'" You can't make people change, but you can give them options that encourage change over time. Some of our students learned needed skills; others developed the confidence needed for success; and still others learned to take advantage of other resources available to them. Providing long-term assistance may cost us something, but the rewards far outweigh the cost.

Jesus concluded his parable by urging the lawyer to "go and do likewise." He encourages us to do the same. We want a system of rules. Jesus gives us attitudes of mercy and compassion that express themselves in action to help others. It doesn't matter who *they* are. The true indicator is who *we* are. Will we be neighbors by showing Christ's love and mercy to those around us?

Serving can be impersonal

How often was one of our students told by a governmental agency to call at a particular time for the help she needed, only to spend hours on hold knowing that, if she hung up, she'd have to start the process all over again? How many sat all day in a health clinic without seeing a doctor? And how often did one wait in line in an office only to hear that nothing could be done about the problem she was facing? "It's policy," was often the answer to any request for flexibility.

It is possible, in fact it's all too easy, for a ministry to become as impersonal as a government agency. There are two ways to do urban ministry—tucked safely behind a desk, or face-to-face with human need. Unfortunately, as you discover if you work with large organizations, the people who can make the decisions that could improve a situation usually are sitting behind desks, sometimes in other parts of the city, while those who deal daily with a hurting world have little power to change procedures or even make exceptions. That may be why many of the policy-makers I've known have been wonderful, caring people who are just a little too far from the trenches to have a lot of impact on what happens there. They may want their front-line staff to be helpful and kind, but they know little about the reception needy people experience when they come in or call. And those front-line staff workers, faced with a never-ending parade of needs they are powerless to meet, may become discouraged and form shells which distance them from the very people they're there to help.

From my experience directing Life Skills Lab, I found that the longer an organization exists the more organized it has to become. There are more paperwork, more figures, more procedures, more files—leaving less time to work directly with the people in need. It's easy to lose sight of Jesus' example of service. Jesus touched people. He got up close and personal with them, and he wants us to do the same.

I prepare to teach class

Fortunately, though it certainly didn't seem so at the time, I was forced to step out from behind my desk and into the classroom the second year classes met. The first of August, 1998, Ruth had extensive foot surgery. She wouldn't be able to stand for some time, and she felt she couldn't teach if she wasn't able to walk around the classroom. I searched for a replacement, but the elders wanted me to take the class. One of them, Bernie James, worked with me to reduce my other responsibilities. I spent the month of August watching the videos, reading the workbooks, and writing lesson plans so I could teach as long as Ruth needed me to.

At the end of August, we tested prospective students in vocabulary and reading comprehension to see how well they read and understood English. We tested seven women the year I taught. Another year, a woman stopped in the middle of taking the comprehension test and told me she needed to go to the adult school and take an ESL (English as a Second Language) class before coming to us. I was glad she recognized

her need, but we never actually failed anyone. We used the tests mostly to give us an idea of the proficiency level of the students and how
we could best help them learn.

Early in September I cleared out the storage cabinet and file cabinet, inventoried supplies and made a list of the materials needed for the
class. Flyers announcing the class were prepared and distributed to
schools, local agencies and libraries. Then we set up the classroom and
purchased supplies.

Computer experts had worked long hours to have the new computers ready. We had arranged tables on three walls of a narrow classroom, put a lock on the door, and installed the new computers to make
a computer lab. What a relief to have all the computers set up and available for classes. All we lacked was a teacher for the lab. Judye had had
to take a full-time job, so she wasn't available.

One night at my care group meeting, Josan suggested that a friend
of hers, a lawyer with young children who was in Los Angeles while her
husband completed his hospital internship, might be interested. April
Key was an excellent addition to the staff. She put together study book-
lets, made a personalized binder for each woman with a pocket for her
own floppy disk, and expressed a real interest in each student.

I get to know the students

On the first day of class, I wrote in the journal I kept in the classroom
while the students wrote in theirs: "Carla and Cindy seem to dominate
the class. Linda is my other talker. Monique is quiet, and Marta is almost
painfully shy. I hope I can draw Marta out and get Carla and Cindy to
step back just a little."

Betty joined the class the next day. She had read about it in the
newspaper. Dora came after she got her son enrolled in kindergarten.
She had failed to take him for the shots he needed to start school. When
the principal at La Ballona called and asked us to add Juana, we were
up to eight students. Juana already had a job with the school, but she
needed computer skills to keep it. I was sorry she'd miss the job training curriculum, but I let her come just for computer lab. It would give
her the skills she needed for the job she already had and would help
the principal, who had been very supportive of our program.

We study about Jesus

Every morning, the class began with a devotion. The students took turns reading from the book of Mark using the Contemporary English Version of the Bible. Then they discussed the reading, prayed and wrote in their journals.

Mark tells the story of Jesus, the basis of our faith, and is short enough to be covered in the ten weeks of class. It emphasizes Jesus' acceptance of everyone, especially women and sinners. Most of the women in the classes felt worthless and plagued by guilt. They blossomed as they read of Jesus' love and forgiveness.

We used the Contemporary English Version because most of our students didn't read well, and many weren't native English speakers. The CEV was easier for them to read and understand than other versions. The students were surprised that they could understand the Bible, a book they'd regarded with an almost superstitious awe as beyond their comprehension.

Marvin and I began by praying for the students, but as soon as they felt ready, we encouraged them to pray. We told them that prayer is just talking to God, and they could say anything they wanted to him. Students from a Catholic background especially appreciated this less formal approach to prayer.

Not long after the class began, I taught my usual session on three forms of journaling, handing out inexpensive black-and-white Comp Books to use as journals and giving the students time to practice each of the forms. We did *exploratory journaling*—exploring our lives in the present, going wherever our thoughts took us; *meditative journaling*— meditating on scripture or writing prayers; and *growth journaling*— looking back over our lives to see how far we've come. After laying that foundation, we let the students write whatever they wanted each morning. Their journals weren't graded. Nobody read a student's journal but the student herself.

Before the first class had ended the previous fall, the students began asking to buy their Bibles. We had purchased them in bulk and were able to sell them for the $3 we'd paid for each. It was the only thing the students were ever asked to pay for. It might seem strange to charge for a Bible, but they weren't expensive, and paying indicated that the student was more likely to be serious about Bible study. Years after they took the class, graduates would tell me that they were still reading their Bibles, praying and journaling.

We study the Adkins curriculum

The class had two major parts—the computer lab for specific skills training, and the classroom for job preparation. The Adkins curriculum developed at Columbia University was Ruth's choice for us to use in the job preparation part of the program. It began each week with a stimulus video, a dramatized situation that illustrated the point of that week's lesson. The video was followed by a discussion designed to draw out the class members and help them apply their knowledge and experience to the situation they'd just seen. That's a major difference between teaching children and adults. Children may not know about a subject until they have studied it, but adults have experiences that can be brought to bear on the topic of getting a job. Some suggested approaches to avoid, while others shared approaches that had worked for them or people they knew. Both were helpful. They allowed the students to supplement each other's knowledge and showed them how their own experience could be applied to problems they were facing.

After watching and discussing the video, the students worked in workbooks filled with practical information and learning activities. At the end of each week, they made an oral report on what they had learned. We videotaped their presentations so they could observe themselves speaking and catch any behaviors that might distract from their message. After ten weeks of presentations, they were comfortable speaking about their abilities and interests and ready to interview effectively for a job. The curriculum enabled them to improve their reading, writing, speaking and listening skills while gaining self-confidence.

Many of the women had been assured by their husbands or boyfriends that they didn't need to work, or even go to school. "Just stay at home and raise the children. I'll take care of you. It's the man's place to support the family," he'd say. But a few years later, the men, discouraged and overextended, would leave those women with families of two or three children and neither the experience nor the education to provide for them. Many had been abused by their fathers, husbands or boyfriends. Their self-confidence needed a big boost for them to be able to present themselves with poise and assurance to a prospective employer.

We supplement the curriculum

At first the class included two field trips—one to a local library to research various careers and one to the One Stop, the City of Los Angeles job placement agency, to sign up for their services. Later classes took a third trip to nearby West Los Angeles College to sign up for the advanced training required for such popular careers as child care and nursing. West Los Angeles is a community college, and most of our graduates were able to attend without charge.

The second week of class, I became aware of the need to talk about professionalism in the classroom. After the students overcame their initial fear, some behaved like children, talking and running and being boisterous when I stepped out of the room. I needed to set a more professional tone if I hoped to prepare them for the workplace. The students needed to be more serious and do their work, whether anybody was watching them or not.

The first week's curriculum encouraged the students to examine themselves—their interests, skills and values—to determine the kinds of jobs they were best suited for. The second week they looked at the work world to see what kinds of jobs were available, what the requirements were for those jobs, how to get into them, what the salary range and working conditions would be, and what the chances were for advancement. To supplement the text, we went to the library so they could research their potential careers in the *Occupational Outlook Handbook* and online. From Monday through Thursday the students studied the job training curriculum, which included videos, workbooks, special speakers, and student presentations. On Wednesday afternoons, Jenny Ricker led a group counseling session, and on Thursday mornings, Ron Lau taught money management. Computer lab met on Fridays. April taught computers, with help from several members of the congregation who were knowledgeable about computers and able to take a morning or afternoon off work to help. Pride Joseph did computer support, keeping the hardware functioning.

The students arrived at 9 a.m., and we began each day with Bible study and prayer. Then they wrote in their journals, and we began job preparation training. Each student was assigned a mentor.

Most of the students were single moms. Many were referred by the Family Center at nearby La Ballona Elementary School. One came because of a newspaper article; and one was a Culver Palms member. We were encouraged by their response to Life Skills Lab. The students loved it and were grateful to the volunteers. Several commented on how much they enjoyed studying the Bible. Cindy brought her children to worship regularly and sat with her mentor.

We cope with challenges

Dora was an exception to the general rule that the students loved and appreciated their classes. She was negative and wouldn't stop talking—to me and to others—while I was trying to teach. She was high strung and had trouble concentrating and taking instruction. She and Betty were the only African-American students in a class full of Hispanics. She lost no opportunities to let the Hispanic students know how superior she felt.

I became so frustrated with her that I spoke with Bernie James, one of our elders, about her. He told me to be patient and not confront her, but accept her, giving her time to adjust. Thanks to his encouragement, the next time she disrupted the class, I was able to regain order without getting angry. I was grateful when the students, especially Cindy and Dora, helped me celebrate my birthday later in September.

The third week, the students made career choices based on their study of themselves and the job market. By that point most were getting discouraged, and a couple were ready to give up. It was a typical pattern: the students would start out intimidated by the experience, then as they grew more comfortable in class, all sorts of negative feelings emerged—about the class, about themselves, about their home situations and upbringing. We'd discuss their concerns, pray about them and write in our journals. I asked God to help me find ways to meet the needs of each student, to be firm but kind, wise but not a know-it-all, helpful but not enabling. I needed to help the students, in Ruth's words, to be independent and interdependent—to encourage each other as they learned to provide for themselves.

The fourth week they learned about contacting prospective employers. They discussed people they could ask and places they could check for job leads. I brought in want ads and telephones for them to practice making calls to inquire about openings. They drafted business letters requesting information or application forms, and typed them in the computer lab. The economy was beginning to sour, and I was concerned that they might not be able to find jobs. I was getting tired, particularly of trying to get Dora to be quiet and cooperate and learn. Still, it was a blessing to be able to teach. Some of the best times I had were in the classroom. I was grateful for the privilege as well as the challenge of influencing the students' lives in such a direct way. One day, one of the students asked me how I managed to maintain such a calm and quiet spirit. It wouldn't last.

I lose control

Near the end of the fifth week, I totally lost control in class. I could read curricula, digest it and pass it on, care about the women and want to help them grow, even inspire them to reach toward God. But I was weak on classroom management. The students had so many stresses it wasn't surprising that tempers flared. And I knew it was a risk to keep Dora in the class. She constantly fanned the flame of any dispute.

That day, Cindy complained that I was favoring Dora. I had to keep myself from laughing. Dora struck back, then Carla jumped in. I told everybody to be quiet, and everyone but Dora was. She just kept talking, even while I was telling her to stop. I lost my temper and started to tremble. Marvin took me out of the classroom, and I ended up sobbing into his shirt. "I *told* the elders I wasn't a teacher." When I collected myself and returned to the classroom, Marvin took Cindy and then Dora out for one-on-one talks. Marvin works as a chaplain for the Probation Department and has excellent counseling skills. That's an important asset in urban ministry.

When I let my feelings come out, it was as if a dam broke. The students suddenly felt freer to talk about their problems. That day, they discussed several issues they hadn't shared before, including sexual abuse.

Ministry is messy business. It not only serves people with very real problems, it is carried out by people with very real problems. If you're trying to hide your problems and weaknesses, don't go into urban ministry. It will bring you face to face with them every time. Ministry holds a mirror to our faces, and the reflection isn't always flattering.

When I got back to the office after class, I called Bernie again. He encouraged me to drop Dora for the good of the rest of the class, but he left the decision up to me. I was afraid it was her last chance, as her

benefits were scheduled to be cut that March. I said I'd give her a warning if she disrupted the class again and let her go if it happened a third time.

A law professor at Pepperdine, Bernie pointed out that you can
teach, but you can't control the process. I knew he was right. I also
knew that I felt too great a need for control in the classroom. I needed
to lighten up and trust God—and the students—more.

I share with other teachers

The next weekend, I was scheduled to speak for the Urban Ministry
Conference in Memphis on "Building Bridges from the Church to Its
Local Community." It was hard to think of teaching others when I still
had so much to learn. I was learning that urban ministry isn't easy.
Personalities are the hardest part. Mixed-race groups create extra tensions. Different styles and personalities are needed to bring out the best
in people. I couldn't do it, but God could do it through me. I needed
to give up pride and control and let him use me to be really successful.

When I got to Memphis, I was eager to talk with people from other
ministries about their programs—to pick their brains about incorporat-
ing both church and community people as students and volunteers,
about maintaining control in the classroom without being heavy-handed,
about helping students without doing things for them that they could do
themselves, about controlling anger when people seemed to be using
the program to extend their welfare payments. (That only happened in
three cases out of 71 students we graduated.)

When I got home, I prayed that everyone who was in Memphis
received a blessing from having been there. I thanked God for my contact with other Life Skills Lab teachers, for the classes I attended and the
chance I had to share. I was grateful for the old friends I saw and the
new friends I made, and I prayed that I had blessed them as much as
they blessed me.

I look at the people

Upon returning to Life Skills Lab, I was able to look with new eyes at
the people in the classroom. What did I see? I saw Marvin, always helpful,
ever wise, pointing out another perspective. I saw Dora, full of anger
and drive, wanting to do and be something special, yet ending up being
her own worst enemy. Carla, coming out of an abusive home situation,

but wanting to be a good mother, making big changes in her life. Betty, wise and capable, yet wounded by a traumatic experience on her last job. Cindy, driven and eager, trying to act tough. And Marta, shy and intimidated, but growing in confidence.

The class finished unit 6, on time management, and 7, on developing short- and long-term career plans, before the end of October. There were just three more units to go. Dora was still a problem, but we managed to avoid further blow-ups for a time.

We throw a party

At the end of the month, the staff and mentors gave a Halloween party for the children of the students. My daughter Kathy baked cookies, and I made sandwiches. April helped set up, and Cathy Somar and her daughter Petra brought cupcakes and costumes to add to those we'd borrowed from other members of the congregation. The students began arriving even before the mentors did, and they pitched in to help. Cathy started face painting. April made punch. And Keith brought candy to fill bags for the children to take home.

We had plenty of food—including fruit and fresh veggies—and plenty of face paint. We were just short one costume, and Kathy and Josan picked that up. It was a special evening, and the children of our students had a blast.

Parties, holidays, birthday celebrations, potluck dinners with the class members bringing their native foods—even just encouraging notes on the chalkboard meant a lot to our students. Rosa Spivey, whose family helped set up for classes each week, occasionally put flowers or small containers of candy at each student's place. Most of them weren't accustomed to such special attention.

I ask forgiveness

I had trouble with Dora one more time before the class ended. She overstepped the bounds and wanted to take over the class. Marvin and I took her out to talk with her, but, as usual, she was full of denials and excuses. I finally gave up and went back into the classroom. It was too near graduation to drop her now, but I knew her attitude would hurt her on any job she got. I wanted to be able to help her, but all I could do was feel frustrated.

Thinking back over the class to that point, I could see that, although Dora had made things difficult, she wasn't the only problem. I may have seen myself as a good Christian, trying to help the wounded person by the roadside, but I needed some attitude adjustment as well. I needed to be a neighbor to Dora. Instead, I asked another church member to pray for her. As often happens when we ask for prayers for others, I ended up gossiping about her. I was the lawyer, seeking to justify myself, not the Good Samaritan, showing mercy to someone damaged by life.

I prayed for forgiveness for my lack of love. I asked God to help me keep my mouth shut and to change my heart so that, when I did open my mouth, what came out would be kind.

The next week, when we started unit 8 on applications and resumes, Betty, who used to train nurses, talked privately with me about my teaching. She said that in a classroom setting, the students, even though they're adults, tend to revert to the behavior patterns of children. For that reason, and to help create good workplace habits, it's important to establish rules immediately. Rules should include: no talking while someone else is talking, no talking during class time about matters that aren't the subject of discussion at the time, no whispering or note-passing, be quiet and continue working if the teacher has to leave the room, no swearing or offensive language, conduct yourself as a professional at all times, over five absences that aren't related to getting a job means you won't get a certificate, participate in class discussions, don't leave the room except to go to the restroom. If a break is needed for coffee or to use the phone, request it for the entire class. Come into the classroom promptly at 9 a.m. Lunch break begins at 12 noon and ends promptly at 12:30. You shouldn't have to be reminded.

I wished I'd posted those rules before the class began. It could have saved me a lot of grief.

The class winds down

I felt discouraged—about my abilities as a teacher and about the way some of the students were responding. I probably shouldn't have admitted Dora, or should have let her go when Bernie suggested it, but by this point it seemed too late. She seemed to be making an effort, and I knew she'd be hurt if she didn't graduate with the rest of the class.

In mid-November, we started unit 9 on interviews, and the students finished their resumes. As the last week neared, I had mixed emotions. It was bittersweet to come to the end of my first experience teaching Life Skills Lab. I hadn't wanted to do it, and it was the hardest thing I'd ever done, but I knew I'd miss it when it ended.

I used the final week to pull all our learning together. I prayed that God would let graduation be a special event for the graduates and their families. I prayed that he'd be with each student and help her build the career she needed. I prayed that those who worked with the program would feel good about their accomplishments and want to help again. And I prayed that the women had come to know God and would choose to follow him. I asked him to bless them and strengthen them and help them succeed.

The students filled out evaluations on the class. All were favorable except Dora's. I hoped our difficulties hadn't hurt the other students. I hoped they had benefited from the class and learned to examine themselves, to get along better with others, and to gain new skills. I knew I had.

Graduation was held the week before Thanksgiving. It was a great party, with plenty of food and a good program and lots of family members and friends. The graduates were happy and excited—even Dora, who made the decorations.

I was so proud of the graduates. After the devastating earthquake, Carla returned to Honduras to help with relief. Cindy went to work in a doctor's office and later applied for a job with the police force. Linda married a fine man who loved and took care of her and her children. Monique was hired as a page at the library and received several subsequent promotions. Marta worked as an aide at Cedars-Sinai Hospital. She attended West Los Angeles College where they helped her overcome a learning disability. Betty got a job with PATH (People Assisting the Homeless) and went back to school to study social work. Juana worked for the school district for several years and referred her sister, Inez, to Life Skills Lab. The last I knew, Dora hadn't gotten a job.

I learned several things from teaching Life Skills Lab:

1. That including devotions in the daily schedule was helpful to both students and staff. We all need a spiritual focus as we start our day.
2. That there is no substitute for a good curriculum.

3. That God provides what's lacking in us.
4. That it's important to set rules early and maintain a professional atmosphere in the classroom.
5. That we can't help everyone.
6. That we can't always be in control, but losing control isn't all bad. It can help others be more open about their problems.
7. That volunteers are the most valuable part of any program.
8. That we can benefit from both pleasant and unpleasant experiences.
9. That most people really do want to succeed.
10. That I could learn from the students.

I prayed that I would learn to see the people around me through God's eyes. He loves all of us—even the most difficult—and he wants what's best for us. He wants us to help people and not try to keep a distance from them. He wants to help us be good neighbors and show mercy to those who have been damaged by life.

Questions for Discussion

1. How can you show mercy to people in need using the pattern of the Good Samaritan?

2. What can we do to keep our Christian ministries in close personal touch with the people we serve?

3. What are the benefits of keeping a spiritual journal?

4. How can we share more deeply and honestly with those we serve?

5. How can we serve others without making them dependent on us? How can we teach independence and interdependence?

CHAPTER 10

Sustaining the Program

Not long after we incorporated Life Skills Lab, Gloria and I sat at the feet of one of the best fund raisers either of us had ever known. There was a time when Norvel Young, past president of Pepperdine University, woke up every morning needing to raise $1,000 that day just to keep the university afloat. And he achieved that aim. When we visited him, he had suffered a stroke and had slowed down considerably from the fast moving, fast talking, hearty man I'd known in my years at the college and with *20th Century Christian* magazine.

He may have moved and spoken more slowly, but his mind was no less alert. We filled pages with notes. We had asked for an hour of his time. He gave us two.

Perhaps the most helpful thing Norvel told me while we were with him was that you need to give money, serious money, to a cause before you can ask other people to give. He was right. After I started making a $1,000 contribution each year to Life Skills Lab, it was much easier to ask other people to do the same.

He gave us three other guidelines:

1. *Never apologize for asking people to give.* God expects all of us as his people, and people in general, to give, and give generously. Fundraising is merely giving people an opportunity to do God's will in regard to their possessions. There are a lot of opportunities out there. People won't necessarily choose yours, but you need to give them the option.

2. *Never decide that someone can't afford to give.* You can't judge what another person can do. Your part is to lay the opportunity before them and let them decide.

3. *Never accept just money.* People have other things to give—prayers, good will, volunteer time, in-kind gifts. In-kind gifts are goods or services—computers, supplies, technical assistance—that are not money but that keep you from having to spend money. Give people a choice of ways to contribute.

Asking people to give money had been difficult for me. I had no problem asking them to give time and energy, or to use their spiritual gifts and creativity. But money seemed different. It might have had something to do with the unusual regard we as Americans have for it. You can borrow an egg from a neighbor without thinking of returning it, but a dollar is a different matter. And yet asking for money was just what we needed to do.

It's one thing to start a wonderful, life-changing program. Everyone is interested in each success, everyone wants to help, and it seems that God is right there, leading the way. But it's quite another thing to keep it going. The initial excitement begins to wear thin, supporters fall by the wayside, and resources of time, money, people, materials and energy may not stretch far enough to cover the needs. Gradually, even the sense of God's immediate presence seems to fade. It appears as though, if you don't hunker down and do something fast, all your successes will come to naught.

Irving R. Warner wrote:

> Fund raising is an art. Comparing it to painting, sculpture, or music may be carrying it too far, so let's try cooking. Almost anybody can prepare a nourishing meal, even if it means opening a dozen cans to do it. Anyone who can read can follow a recipe from a cookbook. Fund raising has recipes, too. It has techniques and practices you can learn just as you can learn to fold an egg into batter or how to stuff a turkey. You'll never become an artist if you don't master them, and you'll never become an artist if all you learn are techniques to which you become a slave.[1]

Early Christians gave to meet needs

The early Christians cared about other people and their well-being. In a description of their activities in the book of Acts, we see that they sold their own possessions to be sure that everyone's needs were met (Acts 2:44-45).

The writer of the book of Acts tells us that

all the believers were one in heart and mind. No one claimed that any of his possessions was his own, but they shared everything they had....There were no needy persons among them. For from time to time those who owned lands or houses sold them, brought the money from the sales and put it at the apostles' feet, and it was distributed to anyone as he had need (Acts 4:32-35).

The account continues with the example of Barnabas, who sold a field he owned and contributed the proceeds from the sale to meet the needs of others.

As Ron Sider wrote:

Acts 4 underlines the evangelistic impact of their trans- formed economic relationships. Verse 32 describes their sweep- ing economic sharing, and the very next verse adds, "And with great power the apostles gave their testimony to the resurrec- tion of the Lord Jesus." Jesus' prayer that the loving unity of his followers would be so striking that it would convince the world that he had come from the Father has been answered—at least once! It happened in the Jerusalem church. The unusual quali- ty of their economic life together gave power to the apostolic preaching.[2]

We see a similar generosity in the contribution Paul collected from Gentile churches to support the poor saints in the church at Rome. Sharing possessions was as much a part of the life of the early church as sharing worship, encouragement, and fellowship.

Generosity is a Christian virtue. As Christians, we need to share what we have to help others. Those of us with the means should give to encourage those in ministry. And those in ministry need to make financial contributions so they can grow in this virtue as well. As Christians we are to give all—not all but our money. By our own giving, we set an example and are able, without embarrassment, to ask others to give to support the good works we're involved in.

Funding programs by writing grants

By the end of December, 1999, our Life Skills Lab job training program had a two-year history of service and was poised on the brink of expansion. All that remained was to access the funding we needed to grow. Most of the rest of this chapter is based on a paper on grantwriting that I submitted to Jude Tiersma Watson, associate professor of urban mission at Fuller.[3] I hope it proves helpful to others who need to raise support.

When you start a service project, the first few years are spent developing the program—figuring out what services are needed and how to organize them most effectively to meet your goals. The next few years are spent building a financial base to sustain the program. Most churches can't sustain a complex program like Life Skills Lab, so other sources of financing must be found. A large part of this effort involves grant writing.

Like most specialized efforts, grant writing has a language all its own. In the first few proposals I wrote, when I'd come across a guideline or a request for proposals (rfp) that asked about evaluation, I'd explain how we evaluated student performance in our job training classes. I was shocked to discover that what they were asking for was the way we evaluated the *program itself.* Gradually I came to realize that there were things about grant writing that neither my English degree nor my journalism experience had prepared me for.

Fortunately, both my city government and my seminary came to the rescue. The City of Culver City offered a free training series for nonprofits, and not long after, Fuller sponsored a seminar on "The Church after Welfare Reform." Both were very helpful in preparing me to approach prospective funders on behalf of Life Skills Lab. Meanwhile, in response to my misunderstanding about evaluation, I'd begun calling people to help us figure out how to evaluate the program. We put together a team made up of church and community people to determine what the program should accomplish. Finally, I found a friend who wanted to learn to write grant proposals, and we sat down with the instructions to construct a "boilerplate," or generic proposal, from which we could pull together the material a specific funder requested.

These four elements—the two training sessions, the evaluation process, and actually writing a grant proposal—marked the real beginning of my fundraising experience.

Just before the process was complete, we received our first grant, based on what by that point seemed a really amateurish proposal. Having the generic to draw from gave me confidence that we could respond adequately to funders' requests. But even though the process taught me a lot about grant writing, the most important lesson I learned was that, no matter how well or poorly done, the major strength of a proposal is the program it describes.

The city offers a workshop

In March of 1999, Nancee Lenormand, management analyst for grants for the City of Culver City and an experienced grant writer for non-profits, opened the "Introductory Grants Workshop for the Culver City Inter-Faith Alliance." First, she discussed the special grant funding conditions relevant to religious organizations. I was distressed to discover that 85% of foundations don't give to religious organizations at all, and the remaining 15% that do require a 501(c)(3) to establish a separate non-profit status.[4]

Though the city was particularly interested in helping local religious organizations get funding for youth programs, they were supportive of our efforts to fund our job training program as well. Nancee emphasized the value of collaboration, something I had emphasized since we began planning our program.

Then she walked us through the components of a grant proposal. The first section to be written is the Needs Statement, Needs Assessment, or Description of Target Population. According to Nancee, this is the heart and logic of the proposal. It describes why the project (not the funding) is necessary and includes both touching stories about individuals helped by the program and hard statistics on its results.

The second section is the Objectives section, also called the Ends, Results, Benefits or Aims section. It describes how the project will address the needs presented in the Needs Statement. Goals are broad statements of what a program seeks to achieve. They begin with the word *to*, e.g., "To help people get jobs." Objectives, on the other hand, are expressed in more specific terms. Dick Pancost, a member of our evaluation team, used the acronym SMART (Specific, Measurable,

Appropriate, Realistic and Timed) to test objectives. For example, "Seventy-five per cent of graduates will have jobs within six months of graduation." Both goals and objectives must be clearly tied to the Needs Statement. This is where you identify who is doing what and who is being served.

Next comes the Methods section—how the project will be implemented. It can be called Methodology, Approach, or Project Description. In it, you walk the prospective funder through the project, describing vividly how it works. This section should be very descriptive and visual and may include a time-line. Staffing and staff qualifications should be included, and the section should be sequential and closely tied to the budget.

The fourth section is Evaluation, how the project will be evaluated to determine its effectiveness. This section should tell who will do the evaluation, whether it will be internal or external, the qualifications of the evaluators, the qualifications for success.

The next section, called Future Funding, deals with the sustainability of the project—how funds will be obtained to ensure that the project continues after the grant expires. It should center on a diversified fundraising program and be as specific as possible. Future Funding appears before the budget, as part of the narrative. Other funding sources being sent proposals should be named, and it should be clear that your board is committed to giving themselves and soliciting funds from others.

The sixth section, the Budget, is a financial description of the project. It translates the Methods section into dollars and cents and should include projected and audited financials. The budget should cover the entire project, not just what the proposal is requesting. It should show that income and expenses match. It should include in-kind as well as cash donations, with volunteer hours figured on the basis of an hourly wage as determined by the Department of Labor.

The Conclusion summarizes the proposal and makes the funding request. While the Conclusion is the final section of the proposal, it is not the last part written.

The Introduction is the next-to-last part to be written. It gives background information on the organization, builds credibility and piques interest. It should be interesting, possibly start with a quote, and talk about staff, board and clients. It should also show what the program is accomplishing.

The final part to be written is the Summary, which summarizes the proposal and serves as an abstract or synopsis. It may be very brief, just a paragraph in a short proposal or a page in a longer one. It appears at the beginning of the proposal but is written last. It includes the total cost of the project, funds obtained, and how much is still required. It also states that the organization has its 501(c)(3) tax exempt status.

Other parts of the proposal include the Cover Letter and Appendices. The cover letter is the first piece of information the funder reads. It should state the identity of the group, the support of its board, and the financial request being made. It is never longer than one page and often follows the order of the other components. It may suggest a meeting with the funder, and it is signed by the executive director and the board chair.

Appendices may be included to provide supplemental information. Material furnished in appendices include the IRS determination letter, a list of board members, a brochure, newsletter, or annual report, letters of support, long-range plans, a statement explaining why the organization is unique, a needs assessment or survey, and a list of collaborative partners.

The most immediately helpful handout to me was Mim Carlson's *Winning Grants Step by Step*.[5] From Step 2, "Writing a Compelling Needs Statement" through Step 7, "Preparing the Program Budget," the publication describes the purpose and content of each section, giving tips, samples, and a worksheet with questions about your own program as well as the answers given by a sample program.

Fuller seminar treats welfare reform

"The Church after Welfare Reform: The Exploding Need at Our Doorstep" was a seminar held at the First Congregational Church in Pasadena in April of 1999. It was "designed to help equip faith-based organizations, churches, and community agencies to meet" the needs and opportunities created by the Welfare Reform Bill.

After networking with other providers in the display area, we worshipped together and considered the biblical approach to care for the needy, a historical overview and an assessment of the ability of local faith-based organizations to deal with the problem.

I signed up for two workshops called "Show Me the Money I and

II." In the first workshop, Dr. Jolly Beyioku of the Alliance of Church-Based Community Developers pointed out that "if we say show me the money, our potential funding source will say show us your capacity." Emphasizing the importance of approaching funders from the funders' perspective, Dr. Beyioku encouraged us to demonstrate how strong our organization was to meet the prospective funder's goals.

He pointed out ten elements funders look at in organizations:

1. *Clarity of mission statement*. It can't be too broad or vague, and it must incorporate specific goals.

2. *Organizational leadership*, the relationship between the board and executive director, the frequency of board meetings, minutes to track decisions, and the composition of the board (including community members).

3. *Staff competence* and the ability of the organization to utilize the gifts of staff members.

4. *Stages and steps of the program plan* and implementation strategy, the evaluation process and success rate, and the mechanisms for followup.

5. *Community involvement* and participation in the decision-making process.

6. *Financial control* and reporting—the program budget, balance sheet, audit, accounting, donations and volunteer hours. A strict account should be kept and reported to the board monthly. There should be no co-mingling of funds. This means that churches and agencies must keep separate accounts.

7. *Fundraising plan*. Are there sources for funding beyond the immediate appeal?

8. *Marketing strategy*, both to those being served and to those who help give the service. We need to minister to both groups and have a plan to reach both though newsletters, flyers, local ads, and celebrations.

9. *Working collaborations and partnerships*—relationships with people doing the same thing and with people who complement the program.

10. *Track record*. What is your past performance?

In the second workshop, Sheila Gray of Scribes Technical talked about grant writing. Though her presentation essentially reinforced what I'd learned from the city, she distributed copies of a handy "Proposal Checklist and Evaluation Form" by Norton J. Kiritz.[6]

The second speaker in the workshop, Vance Martin, pointed out how funds from CalWORKs, our state Welfare-to-Work program, were being distributed through already-established channels which left out small programs like ours. Also, CalWORKs emphasized getting people into a job—any job, be it minimum wage or temporary—and training them simultaneously. We trained, then helped our students get jobs. Their program emphasized quantity, ours quality—numbers as opposed to changed lives.

According to an article by Carla Rivera in the *Los Angeles Times*, CalWORKs funding was earmarked for outsources which provided support services—child care, mental health, domestic violence, and substance abuse. According to Rivera, "Millions of dollars in federal welfare-to-work funds have been funneled to California for job training programs, but much of it remains unused, mired in governmental red tape and shifting priorities."[7] Despite our proven record of success in making families independent, child care seemed to be what churches were expected to provide.

Fuller's seminar expanded my knowledge about grant writing while making me more realistic about our chances for success.

We establish an evaluation team

Next, we put together an evaluation team of fifteen members from the church and the community. Maryan Baskin, an experienced evaluator, led us through the process. We met monthly from February through May to set goals and objectives and determine how to ascertain when those goals had been met.

At the first meeting, the group drafted a mission statement:

> The Culver Palms Life Skills Lab seeks to meet the needs of our community by offering training in job and social skills, providing a coordinated system of support, serving the business community, and transforming individuals and their families.

We listed six basic goals we were trying to reach:

1. To develop the ability and confidence of our students to reach the long-term career goals they set for themselves.

2. To make families more stable and self-supporting.

3. To develop the skills needed to interview, obtain, maintain and advance in employment.

4. To develop an awareness of, and skill in using, a variety of resources to acquire needed information about jobs.

5. To encourage graduates to be good-will ambassadors for Life Skills Lab.

6. To provide the local business community with a qualified pool of potential employees.

In the next two meetings, we came up with demonstrable, measurable, and timed objectives that would allow us to meet those goals. For example, for the first goal, to develop the ability and confidence in our students to reach the long-term career goals they set for themselves, we listed the following objectives:

- Of those students who commit to the full program, 80% will graduate.
- On a self-confidence evaluation administered at the end of the program, 90% will indicate that they feel more confident about meeting their long-term goals.
- On a written survey of graduates administered one year after graduation, 80% will say they remain focused on their long-term goals.

We compared the objectives with the units of our curriculum to see which already were being met in the classroom and discussed methods for determining when we'd met the others.

The final month we looked for ways to implement the objectives—particularly those relating to the last two goals, which weren't covered in the curriculum. Plans were made for an alumni follow-up program, including a newsletter, annual events, and opportunities for alumni to speak to later classes. Ways to interact with potential employers were also discussed.

When the evaluation process was complete, the team moved from meeting monthly to meeting every other month, and from evaluation to serving in an advisory capacity. Individuals from the team undertook projects related to the evaluation. One began pushing through the incorporation process so we could get our 501(c)(3), another produced a newsletter to communicate with graduates, and a third volunteered to help with grant writing.

We draft a generic proposal

I was blessed in my areas of ignorance. Talented people always were willing to step in and contribute. As Paul put it, "When I am weak, then I am strong" (2 Corinthians 12:10), because God's grace flows in our weakness.

Perhaps the best example of this principle occurred when I felt I was ready to begin work on a proposal that would incorporate all that I had learned. Meredith, the wife of Phil, our new Life Skills Lab instructor, mentioned that she lost out on a job she really wanted because she lacked grant writing experience. I offered to help her get some by helping me write a generic proposal. She accepted and brought more to the project than I had imagined. Her strengths perfectly complemented my weaknesses.

We followed the outline Nancee had distributed, reading through and working the worksheets to prepare material for each section.

At first, I had trouble confusing the need *for* the program with the needs *of* the program, the goals of our curriculum with the goals of the program overall, the methods of instruction with the methods of meeting our objectives. It was hard enough to prepare a one-year budget, let alone consider where the money was coming from after the grant funds were exhausted (Future Funding), but I soon realized that program sustainability was at least as important as training methods.

The Introduction and Summary sections seemed repetitive and made some of the rest of the proposal repetitive when added to the front, necessitating several rewrites to make it read smoothly. But it was worth it, because the more we rewrote, the clearer things became in our minds. I found the process essential for clarification and goal-setting.

From the resources of our city, my seminary, our church and community, and God who helps us in our weaknesses, I became much more confident in my abilities to write grants and sustain our program, allowing us to train people to support their families for years to come.

We put together an annual plan

To bring in the funding we needed for Life Skills Lab, the elders advised me to stop taking urban ministry classes at Fuller and enroll in fundraising classes offered through UCLA Extension. I signed up for my first class on "The Art of Fund Raising" the end of May. Based on that class, I set up a notebook with annual goals for fundraising through Direct

Mail, Special Events, Foundations/Corporate, Leadership Gifts, Major Gifts, and In-kind Gifts.

I wrote a Direct Mail solicitation letter that brought in $1,880 of the $2,000 I'd anticipated. Special Events brought in a little more than half the $8,000 budgeted based on doubling the money we made on our benefit the previous year. Grants only brought in half the $40,000 I had hoped.

The most successful effort in my first year of fundraising was in the area of Major Gifts. Major Gifts are contributions of $1,000 or more solicited on a personal basis. With a goal of $3,000, we raised $8,000!

Then, at our Thanksgiving turkey distribution, State Assemblyman Kevin Murray asked for a copy of a grant proposal to submit to the legislature. I faxed him the generic proposal Meredith and I had written. That brief conversation in the kitchen of the church building eventually would result in a grant from the State of California.

How do you sustain funding for a program to serve needy people?

*Take advantage of all the sources of information that are available—*informed individuals, printed material, religious and governmental training opportunities.

Enlist others to help with the various aspects of fundraising. I worked with Gloria, Norvel, Meredith, Nancee, Dick, Tom, and David.

*Get the proper documentation to raise funds—*a letter from the IRS stating that you are a 501(c)(3) charity operating for the public good.

Set attainable goals for evaluation. Assemble a group with an experienced leader like Maryan to set goals and measurable objectives for the program.

Approach grant writing from the funders' perspective. What do funders need to know about you to be able to trust you with their money?

Play to your strengths. Recognize that, though you may be competitive with government programs in terms of innovation, personal attention, speed of response and personal transformation, you'll never be able to serve as many people in as short a time.

Don't put all your eggs in one basket. Diversify your fundraising efforts through personal solicitation, direct mail, grantwriting, and special events.

We need to learn to see giving—and asking others to give—through God's eyes as something good for us, good for ministries, and good for the people of the city—people whose lives are made better because those ministries exist.

Questions for Discussion

1. What is the connection between giving and raising funds for good works?

2. What are some current cultural attitudes that make it difficult to ask people to give?

3. Discuss the rationale for the various parts of a grant proposal.

4. Is it important to learn to look at an organization from a funder's perspective? Are there limits to doing that?

5. Why does a ministry need a mission statement, goals and objectives?

CHAPTER 11

Working with Staff & Students

In the summer of 1999, Inez came to us. She had escaped with her two sons from the desert where her husband made, sold, and took drugs. Inez and her sons had come to Los Angeles with just the clothes on their backs. I helped her find clothing from the Back-to-Work Boutique, then signed her up for Life Skills Lab that fall. She wanted to be a bus driver, and she was so determined I knew she would succeed. That summer my mother in Texas was feeling overwhelmed trying to keep up her house there. I flew back to help my sister Barbara clear out the house and move Mother into an assisted care facility. To help with her expenses and trips back and forth to Texas, I took a part-time teaching job with Pepperdine's public relations department. I thanked God for his merciful kindness in providing for our needs and asked for strength to keep up the pace.

The fall class begins

On August 28, we tested students for the fall Life Skills Lab class, which began in September.

While I was holding down two jobs, God sent Rona Kingsley to help in the office, first as a volunteer and then in a half-paid, half-volunteer part-time position. In practical matters, Rona and I are very different. She is accustomed to having and spending money, while I never spent a cent on the program that we didn't already have in hand. But we agreed on one thing: both of us were devoted to Life Skills Lab and worked as hard as we could to make it a success. In the process, we became good friends and allies.

Rona rearranged the office to give us more space and greater efficiency, kept the financial records, did purchasing and managed accounts, and helped with events. An excellent speaker, she emceed most of our programs.

I handled staff supervision, student and volunteer recruitment, fundraising, and disciplinary matters. Then I drove to Malibu two evenings a week to teach public relations classes.

Problems mount

Not long after Life Skills Lab began that September, Ruth Johnson had to quit teaching for us because of her health. How could we keep the class going without her? How could I keep going? Phil McCollum, a graduate student, had been assisting Ruth. By moving April and the computer lab to Mondays, with Phil teaching on Tuesdays, Jenny counseling on Thursday afternoons and my teaching Thursday mornings and all day Wednesdays and Fridays, we covered my Tuesday and Thursday afternoon trips to Malibu and were able to continue offering the class.

The class was about halfway over when Inez's second son, Joshua, had a breakdown and was expelled from public school. Inez had been taking drugs when she was pregnant with him, adding guilt to her other burdens. We both knew that an eight-year-old was supposed to be in school somewhere, but we didn't know how to get him there. The public school wouldn't take him back because he was too disruptive, and Inez didn't have the money for a private school. I turned it over to God and Joshua's counselors at Didi Hirsch Community Mental Health Clinic, praying that Inez would be able to come back to us and that God would strengthen us all.

Our students find success

Jake, our first male graduate, was a recovering alcoholic with a criminal record. While he was in class, he worked with a judge to clear his record, then got a great job at an oil refinery. Edna went into telemarketing, Juanita worked in a hospital supply unit, Jennifer got a job in an office and then started college, and Ying, our Chinese minister's wife, became a lab assistant at UCLA.

We had two more students who did particularly well that year. Carmen, whose English was limited, got her license and opened a child care business in her home. Through connections I had made through SPA5 of the County Children's Planning Council, I was able to refer her to an agency that guided her through the licensing process, all in Spanish. Then another agency took her under its wing, giving her continuing training and referring parents to her newly-licensed Family Day Care Center.

Sabeldi had called to apply after her daughter told her, "When I grow up I want to be just like you." Rather than feeling proud, Sabeldi had burst into tears. She felt her life was going nowhere. She wanted to be a teacher, and she had some computer experience, but she hadn't graduated from high school. While she was studying with us, she helped other students in the computer lab, worked in child care and started working toward her high school diploma. Not long after she finished Life Skills Lab class, she was baptized. We celebrated her high school graduation as a part of the youth ministry party for high school graduates that year, and she enrolled in child development classes at West Los Angeles College. She helped teach children's classes at Culver Palms and was an avid Bible student. Later, we hired her as a computer lab teacher. She was one of our great successes.

Carmen and Sabeldi came to us from the family center at the local elementary school. Eventually, we had a list of almost 30 schools and agencies willing to refer clients to our job training program. Before each new class, we'd visit each of them, taking flyers, brochures, and other information about the class. These trips were designed to nurture our relationships and remind the agencies to use us as a resource for clients and their families who needed jobs.

We learn from Joseph

Health and wealth enthusiasts have tried to convince us that, if we truly are God's children, seeking to serve him and others, our lives will be a smooth progression from success to even greater success. When we're in ministry, we may expect God's presence consistently to comfort and inspire, smoothing out the road before us. Yet, even a cursory glance at scripture indicates that almost the opposite is true. Being God's child and seeking to do his will almost seems to insure hard times. Look at Job, David, even Jesus. But perhaps Joseph is the best example for urban ministers.

Joseph went from the rural life of a Palestinian shepherd to urban ministry on a massive scale in the power-driven capital of Egypt, one of the oldest and most glittering cultures of his time. Rosenblatt calls it "a society not unlike our own: sophisticated, materialistic, rife with intrigue and power politics. Joseph's fidelity to the faith of his fathers manifests through the choices he makes as he ascends to the pinnacle of power in an alien culture."[1]

But it wasn't a sudden elevation—or even a smooth climb. Joseph's life was a series of successes and failures that began in his childhood. The favored son of an old and indulgent father, Joseph was lavished with favors. Even God seemed to single him out for something special.

Whether he bragged about the fact or just passed it on as a curiosity, his ten older brothers didn't respond with equanimity. They tried to get rid of him, first by throwing him into a well, then by selling him to traders bound for Egypt. Things began to look up as Joseph rose in the service of a prominent Egyptian official. That is, until the official's wife had him arrested. Referring to the blood-dipped coat his brothers used to convince their father that Joseph had been killed, and the coat he left with Potiphar's wife as he fled from her embrace, Rosenblatt says, "With yet another coat stripped from his body, it is as if Joseph is repeatedly shedding his skin as he descends from his father's favor into enslavement in Egypt and finally imprisonment."[2]

Joseph goes from depths to heights

Why did God allow Joseph to experience such depths? Rosenblatt believes it was for his own good.

> As Jacob's sheltered favorite son, Joseph never really had a chance to discover the outer limits of his character. Now, as a powerless slave in an alien land, Joseph will be tested on both a physical and a spiritual level. Can he survive in a hostile environment and fulfill his dreams of glory? After the cruel betrayal by his brothers, can Joseph recover his faith in both man and God?[3]

Urban ministry often is discouraging. When the people we serve reject our efforts, when needed funding fails to materialize, when others don't seem to care, or even oppose us, it's easy to feel that God has let us down. Joseph may have felt that way at the bottom of the well, being sold into slavery, languishing for years in prison. But even this low led to new heights when, after years in prison, he was freed to supervise a government food distribution project the likes of which had never been seen before—and seldom since.

"Only after he is stripped of all privileges and sold into slavery does Joseph's strength of character begin to emerge," Rosenblatt points out.[4] In part as a result of his difficulties, Joseph is able to forget himself and sympathize with others.

"Once he emerges from prison," she writes,

Joseph's latent leadership talents come to the fore. The dreamer has now become the man of action. Not only does he display his intuition in deciphering the meaning of Pharaoh's dream, he has the political acumen to conceive a plan for coping with what the dream portends. Joseph doesn't try to pass himself off as a soothsayer or magician, but takes care to credit God as the source of his insights. But he uses his God-given talent of persuasion to get himself appointed to carry out his rescue plan.[5]

Good can come from bad

Rosenblatt emphasizes how Joseph grew from his experiences. "We... see Joseph developing the very characteristics he lacked in his youth: humility and empathy. Instead of taking personal credit for his skills in dream interpretation, he attributes whatever insights he gleans to God, saying, 'Surely God can interpret!'"[6]

As urban ministers we, like Joseph, learn from our own experience of need to sympathize with those in need. We dream of the means of meeting those needs, turning to God for strength and guidance, and crediting God for answers to prayers as we devise plans for ministry. And we use our persuasive powers to enlist others to help with the project.

God gave Joseph the gifts he needed to perform the tasks God had for him to do. Lewis Drummond says that God has gifted each of us as well. How can we determine what our gifts are? He gives what he calls the "Ten Commandments of Discovering Your Gift"[7]:

1. Have faith that you have one or more gifts. The Bible says you do.

2. Study the Scriptures and what they say about the gifts: (1) Come to understand from the Bible the nature of God's mission in the world. What does he actually want his people to do to cooperate in his mission? (2) Attempt to understand the actual nature of the gifts as recorded in the Scriptures.

3. Ask: How has God truly used me in the past, not just what jobs have I done in the church?

4. Ask: What do spiritual people say (personal testimony, group fellowship)? Often others can help you discover your ministry.

5. Ask: What do I like to do? I like to exercise my abilities. That may well be your "gift," as Stedman pointed out.

6. Ask: What burdens me? True burdens are placed by the Spirit of God. The Holy Spirit may have equipped you to meet those needs.

7. Ask: What challenges me, that is, what does the Holy Spirit lay on my heart? How do I feel led? What does God seem to be saying?

8. Ask: What open doors are before me? What opportunities to ministry are actually open? God may move you to enter that door of ministry, and if he does, he will surely equip you to do it.

9. Rest in Christ. Be open. (1) Do something—keep moving—be disciplined, (2) but be open to change.

10. Prayer and trust is the final exercise. God will reveal his will if you are sincere in seeking his purpose for your life.

I knew I was able to teach and help people. I'd been doing it a long time. I had studied the scriptures on spiritual gifts and even taught a recurring class on them. I enjoyed helping people and I was burdened with the needs of the unemployed single mothers in our area. I felt called to do something about it, and God and the Culver Palms church enabled me to. I prayed and trusted God, but I wasn't very open to change. I thought Life Skills Lab would last forever, and that I would work with it as long as I was able. I saw my major challenge as finding and training someone to carry on the effort after me.

It was an unrealistic expectation. It wasn't God's plan. Unrealistic expectations only exacerbate our problems. If we expect things to go a certain way, if we expect them to continue unchanged, we may be dis-appointed. Dry spells and disappointments come to everyone. "What we learn from Joseph's experience," Rosenblatt says,

> is that if we can survive life's dry spells—whether emotional, financial, or professional—the wheel of fortune will eventually spin around again. But first we must survive. Joseph accepts his life in its totality, its good times and its bad. Because life has so much meaning for him, Joseph feels responsible for making the right choices, regardless of his circumstances. As long as he believes that what he chooses to do matters—even in prison, in a foreign land far from his family—despair will never over-whelm him.[85]

Meanwhile, Inez was still at home, taking care of Joshua. I wanted to help her. I had met Dr. Eli Lefferman of Vista del Mar Child and Family Services when I worked with SPA5. When nothing else seemed to work for Joshua, I asked Dr. Lefferman to admit him to the school and residential facility at Vista. I assured him that, if they took Joshua and let Inez finish her training with us, she would get a job and be able to care for her family. Joshua was accepted at Vista.

We get a new teacher

Phil McCollum became the new Life Skills Lab instructor in the spring of 2000. That was the first year we were able to offer two classes instead of just one in a school year. Having more classes not only enabled us to serve more students, it also helped us have classes available when the need arose. The unemployed people we helped often lived on the edge. By the time they came to us, they couldn't wait eight months for the next class to start. They needed help immediately.

Phil was committed to urban ministry. He had a special interest in church planting, and was learning Spanish to be able to minister to this fastest-growing part of our population. He had studied education and was a gifted teacher. And he had grown up with a single mother, so he related well with our students and their special needs.

Six students started the spring class of 2000. I was thrilled to have Inez back now that her son was at Vista. I offered to let her take up with this class where she'd had to leave the previous one, but she wanted to get everything she could from the experience. She started again at the beginning. I was proud of her drive and determination.

Motivation was the primary determining factor in the success of our students. When we recruited students for the program, I was able to assure the schools and agencies we worked with that, if they sent us motivated people, people who wanted to work and support their families, we would help them get a job.

I prayed that the students in this class would draw together in love and concern, and that we would inspire them with God's Word and teach them the skills they needed to succeed. But again, things didn't work out the way I'd hoped. One woman wasn't really interested in getting a job, another had to drop out and get a stop-gap job to stay afloat, a young male student wore himself out working nights as a security guard and studying with us during the day, and the husband of the fourth didn't want her to get a job.

I was surprised to discover how many men felt threatened by the thought that their wives or girlfriends might be successful. It was one of the greatest obstacles faced by the women we served.

We get help promoting the program

While I was teaching at Pepperdine, I had met Stan Thomas from the college's audiovisual department. Stan had been a missionary in Africa. He volunteered to donate the time and materials to make a video of Life Skills Lab that we could use to recruit students and raise money.

We started the video as the spring class began, taking footage in the classroom and computer lab, then going to the homes and offices of several volunteers to interview them. Fortunately, we'd been able to get most of the classroom shots when the class was larger. With just two students remaining, the elders discussed shutting the class down. I was relieved when they reconsidered. I especially wanted this class to continue for Inez's sake. She had gone through a lot to be able to return to us. I was sure she was motivated to succeed.

Our students triumph

The tiny class had a one hundred per cent success rate. Sonya, whose sister Carmen had opened the child care center, wanted to go into physical thereapy. We paired her with Kelly Shaw, a mentor who was a physical therapist at a local hospital. Kelly encouraged her to train as a physical therapy assistant. Sonya got a job at a local clinic as soon as she finished her training.

Inez struggled to get her bus driver's license, then qualified for air brakes and to transport disabled children. She called to share news of each milestone. First, she drove a bus for ERAS Center, the second of our graduates to work at that center for the developmentally disabled. Before long, she was helping teachers with the children after she brought them to school in the mornings and before she took them home in the afternoons. Then, she was hired to drive for Vista del Mar, the school her son attended. A few years later, she was promoted to Parent Partner with an office of her own and a salary as large as mine! By that time, her son was living at home and doing well in public school. I was especially thrilled for Inez's achievements, knowing how far she'd come.

Family matters

Seeing Sabeldi, Carmen, Sonya, Inez and other graduates who were doing so well, I was convinced that God truly was with us and guiding our efforts. But it was hard to be in California when I felt that my mother and sister needed me in Texas. When I was there, I was concerned about what was happening here. I felt really pulled, but I was grateful that Phil was teaching the class so I could leave when I needed to. I prayed for help to know what my priorities should be and how I should spend my limited time.

I took an inventory of how I did ministry. Sometimes it seems like a waste of precious time to stop and evaluate, but it can be very helpful. It's too easy to get caught up in what we're doing and forget to consider how we're doing it.

Some of the questions and my answers were as follows:

1. *What are my deepest motives for being involved in ministry?* Wanting to help people, to be accepted, to serve and glorify God, to make friends, and to work together as a group toward a common goal.

2. *What are my values?* I value honesty, hard work, and people who do what they say they will.

3. *What are my attitudes?* That ministry is a privilege, that God is in control and will work things out, that bad things do happen, but that

we can work together to make things better—basically optimistic, a little naive, trusting.

4. *What are my assumptions?* That God loves me, that most people at least like me, that Christians want to help people.

5. *What are my experiences?* Christianity, family, journalism, benevolence, outreach, and cross-cultural relations.

6. *What are my strengths?* I'm a self-starter, a hard worker, and a creative thinker. I care about people.

7. *What are my weaknesses?* I get too absorbed in tasks and fail to be kind, aware of other people.

8. *What is enjoyable about work?* People working together for a common goal, feeling needed.

9. *What is not enjoyable?* Being let down, too many demands, no time to reflect.

10. *What gives me energy?* Worship, being with people.

As I took the survey, I realized that some of my motives were selfish and unworthy and that I was wasting valuable energy worrying about whether other people were carrying out their responsibilities. I'd been taking up the slack rather than just letting them take responsibility if they didn't follow through.

I was naive and needed to be more realistic about people and their weaknesses—the people we served, the people we served with, and myself. Urban ministers need to be aware of and guard against the tendency of all people-helpers to become enablers, doing for others what they should be doing for themselves. I needed to learn to do my work with greater joy and peace, to avoid worried striving, and to relax in God and his will.

We receive a special gift

That February my sister called and asked if I wanted to talk with Mother. "Can she really talk?" I asked, dreading another disappointment. The last time I'd seen her she didn't know who I was. When she came on the line, I was astonished at the strength and enthusiasm in her voice. She not only knew me, but she expressed a real interest in my life, and she told me how she was doing. She couldn't remember much that had happened between Thanksgiving and February. I asked her if she remembered that I had been there when she was in the hospital at Christmas.

"I thought you were," she said, and I could hear the smile in her voice.

I was so grateful. We had our mother back. I had asked God to make her clearheaded if he kept her alive, and I was overwhelmed by his answer. It humbled me to realize how little I understood about prayer. I thanked and praised God for allowing us to experience this miracle of his grace.

Things don't always work out that way. In fact, they seldom do. There's no easy explanation why one person's prayer is answered while another prays just as fervently, and things don't work out. And, of course, the miracle was only temporary. Even Lazarus died again. Still, we were grateful to have her back, if only for a short time.

The next month Barbara called that Mother wasn't expected to live through the night. I left for Texas the next morning, but she died before I got there.

When I got back to Los Angeles, I caught up with the class and got some time to grieve. I thanked God for providing what we needed to pay for the funeral and the expenses of the trip. I was glad I'd been able to help my sister. And I was thrilled when, in the fall of 2000, we graduated nine students, our largest class to that point.

I, like Joseph, had experienced thrilling successes and heartbreaking failures. I knew what it meant to face the limits of my character by being stripped of confidence and control. And I saw God's strength in my weakness.

What are some of the lessons we learn from working with our associates and the people we serve?

- That though we don't always know where God is leading us, it's important just to keep putting one foot in front of the other.
- That God will provide, but it won't necessarily be easy.
- That sometimes the people we're trying to help will end up helping us with their examples of persistence and determination.
- That no one is indispensable, and that God will send a replacement if he wants a work to continue.
- That we survive anything that doesn't kill us.
- That God connects us with the people we need to do his work.
- That sometimes the greatest reward of service is someone else's success.

- That God gives us the gifts we need to do the work he's given us to do.
- That God still works miracles.
- That sometimes we need to stop and take stock, and sometimes we just need to stop.
- That every life is a gift, every life ends, but occasionally God surprises us with a second chance.

Father, Thank you for the wonderful blessings you scatter in our paths. Thank you for the people who have blessed our lives, and for those we've been able to bless. Give us strength for the ups and downs of our journey, and grant us the vision to see your hand in all the events of our lives—both those that encourage us and those that make us sad.

Questions for Discussion

1. What are some of the problems you can anticipate from people you're trying to help in urban ministry?

2. What other challenges—both personal and professional—can you expect to encounter?

3. Talk about the people in your life that have been there when you needed them.

4. How is Joseph's life a good example for ministry?

5. What are some of your gifts? the gifts of those around you?

CHAPTER 12

Working with the Government

A hmad, a young man from India, had come to church seeking help from the benevolence committee. He didn't have a job and was about to lose the room where he had been living. Mack Cuthbertson and Brenda Ball, who were in charge of benevolence, gave him immediate assistance and referred him to me for help getting a job. I let him use the computer in my office to update his resume and the phone to follow up on job leads. I gave him food from the food pantry and advice, like wearing socks for an interview. He had been a computer programmer in India and expected to be hired quickly.

When it didn't work out that way, he enrolled in the spring class. I often reminded prospective students that, if they got a job, they could always leave the class. If they didn't, the time would pass anyway, and they'd be better off using it to get as much training as possible. By the time class began, Ahmad was living on the street. His uncle sent money for a month in a cheap hotel.

At first, Ahmad seemed to be doing pretty well. He doodled in the margins of his class books, but he was bright and seemed to be catching on. His biggest problem was getting back to class on time after breaks and lunch. Then one day, the janitor found him smoking in the men's restroom. There was an empty liquor bottle in the trash. With two infractions at once, we had to let him go.

Early one morning a few days later, our minister called to tell me that the office had been vandalized. I rushed over to meet with the police and was shocked to see racial hate language spray painted in huge letters across the front of the office building and the wall beside it. We felt sure Ahmad had done it. Detective Hunter was assigned to the case, and I told her what I knew about him.

A few days later, I was passing the church building on my way to work when I saw our minister talking with police officers. The church building had been vandalized as well, as had about a dozen other houses of worship and businesses in the area.

Ahmad was being counseled at Didi Hirsch Mental Health Clinic, and I called to find out if he was violent. When I explained our situation, the therapist said Ahmad had beaten his mother. I was old enough to be his mother, and he blamed me for dropping him from the class. For the first time since the program began, I was afraid of one of our students. I felt sick as I drove the few blocks between the church building and home, my eyes sweeping the streets nervously. I didn't want him to know where I lived. I asked God to help me not to be afraid. I needed to know how to deal with the difficult people who came to us for help. I needed to know when we could help people and when we needed to refer them somewhere else.

A few weeks later, Ahmad was in jail, charged with a hate crime. With Ahmad safely in jail, awaiting psychological testing, I was able to relax and concentrate on the rest of the class. Nine students had registered. One had trouble with child care and dropped out the first week. Another had a conflict with his work schedule and left soon after. The two Chinese students were having so much trouble because of their limited English skills that they signed up for ESL classes at the adult school. They arranged their classes so they could continue studying with us. Nina's GAIN worker, the counselor assigned to her by CalWORKs, insisted that she attend their Job Club every afternoon. I asked people in several levels of management to allow her to continue with us, but without success. Nina started dividing her time—studying with us in the mornings and going to Job Club in the afternoons. Rachel's husband had run through the sizable savings she had when they married, then charged massive bills on her credit card, leaving her bankrupt. As the class progressed, she came out of her depression, encouraging the other students in the class and helping them with their work. Her growing confidence encouraged me as well.

Upon graduation Rachel applied for a job at Cedars-Sinai Hospital, distributing food trays to patients. She was one of two of the forty applicants hired for the higher-paying job of discussing menu options with patients. The hospital was in the process of converting to a new computer system. Because of her Life Skills Lab training, Rachel was able to show the nurses how to use the new system.

Nina's GAIN worker called that she had a job. Crediting us with helping her get it, they added Life Skills Lab to their lists of approved job preparation and training programs in the area. No longer would we struggle to keep the students who came to us from GAIN. In fact, they would begin referring students to us.

Questions arise

Ahmad, Rachel and Nina were members of the second class funded by our state grant. A lot of questions arise when an organization affiliated with a church accepts government funding. Will the organization lose its distinctive character? Will the government make unrealistic demands and interfere in the affairs of the church? How can we respect the legally-required separation between church and state while encouraging our students' spiritual development? Those were questions we struggled with in the church and in Life Skills Lab. I was surprised to discover that the government was grappling with them as well.

Several governmental officials had worked with Life Skills Lab almost since its inception. The city council of Culver City had invited us to help form an Interfaith Alliance. More than church/state issues, my questions then concerned working with faith groups outside the Judeo-Christian heritage. How do we work together? Do we always end up with events that reflect the lowest common denominator? Can we pray in Jesus' name?

The last question was answered first. The Culver Palms Church of Christ was on the list of churches to be visited on the first Interfaith Alliance event, a Prayer Walk. Members visited and prayed in a variety of temples and houses of worship. Knowing that people were coming who worshipped false gods, I prayed that what we said and did would be in keeping with God's will. As Bakke put it, "How to distinguish between important issues of faith and neutral issues of different cultures remains an important question for modern urban Christians."[1]

When the group entered the building, the Hare Krishnas were chanting about Krishna. I had planned to say a bland, ecumenical prayer, but when I started, I forgot and prayed, as I always did, in Jesus' name. No one seemed to mind, and I was elected vice president of the Interfaith Alliance.

I met with Steven Monsma of the social science division at Pepperdine. He had written a book on church-state relations and was conducting a study of faith-based nonprofits, including Life Skills Lab. As soon as government funding seemed a live option, I asked him how we could handle our devotions, which we considered basic to the success of the program.

He felt they wouldn't be a problem so long as they were optional. They always had been in a sense, because they were the first half hour of the class day. People who weren't interested just came late. All the students ran late from time to time, so we never distinguished. We just started pointing out that, if people objected, they could come at 9:30 instead of 9.

Business is a challenge

When Life Skills Lab incorporated early in 2001, I went from heading a church ministry to running a small business. Soon after, the elders let me know that the church would begin at the end of that fiscal year to reduce their contribution to the program. In fiscal year 2001-02, they would pay two-thirds of my salary, and in 2002-03, they would pay one-third. After July, 2003, they would no longer contribute funds, though they would continue to supply space for the office, classroom and computer lab. The elders felt that, of all the church's ministries, Life Skills Lab had the best chance of becoming self-sufficient.

I had no business experience, and suddenly there were requirements to meet, records to keep, and accounts to balance. All this was on top of what I considered my primary responsibilities: raising money, helping the people we were serving and supervising employees and volunteers.

When our computer teacher moved away, I hired Sabeldi, a graduate, to teach. She had worked in data entry and helped her classmates in the lab, and she was studying to become a teacher. The only problem was how to pay her. I never wanted to hire anyone just for a grant period. All our efforts had been to help people get stable employment. How could we offer less?

Our numbers for the spring class, 2001, were lower than I had expected. Out of 27 who had indicated an interest, ten started the class. The elders were concerned. They asked for statistics in spreadsheets, an unfamiliar computer skill to me. I tend to fear authority figures and I get defensive. I needed to be a better administrator, to organize my work more effectively, and to work better with the board.

I find help

I contacted the Executive Services Corps, an association that matches retired executives with nonprofits that need help. I asked for skills, but Stan Gortikov gave me what I needed even more. He built my self-esteem, which helped me handle criticism better. The next year, Victor Deutsch, a former chief financial officer, became my second coach from Executive Service Corps. He updated our chart of accounts to clarify our financial reports and helped us prepare for a state audit.

I called Memphis Area Community Services (MACS) for their retention figures and the numbers of students in the classes they'd served. Their first five years' figures ran about the same as ours, then quickly rose into the 20s for each class after that. Sabeldi helped me prepare a spreadsheet on recruitment and retention.

Of the ten students who started the spring class, two dropped out the first week. They lived in a shelter and had emotional problems. Three were young pregnant women from a Catholic adoption residence. We worked out a schedule to allow for each delivery. Three had been referred by the Chinese congregation. We had had at least one Chinese student in each class since the second one, and though they had trouble with English, they picked up a great deal and got good jobs, often in labs assisting Chinese-speaking scientists. It was hard to know how much English they had mastered, because they were shy and hesitant to use their English for fear of embarrassing themselves.

We taught them to maintain eye contact in an interview; they'd stare at their feet as a way of showing respect. Before the class ended, the best English speaker of the three had returned to China for a family emergency. I looked for new sources for students, especially to the east and south of our area, where the need was greatest.

I learn to run a business

We filled in and submitted the forms to the IRS to become a 501(c)(3) tax exempt charity, and I attended a seminar by the state Employment Development Department (EDD) on how to figure payroll taxes. That was the hardest part for me. I just seemed to glaze over. I asked a friend, Betty Bridges, a former bank officer from the Vermont Avenue Church, for help. She and her sister Josephine Downs, an accountant, volunteered to handle payroll taxes without charge. They figured what we owed each employee, as well as the federal government (IRS) and the state (EDD). All I had to do was write the checks.

We purchased liability insurance and workers compensation. Life Skills Lab didn't qualify, but the firm in San Diego that handled the church's insurance qualified us on the basis of the church's record.

We had kept financial records on the computer since January, 2000, thanks to the heroic efforts of David Hwa. But David was being transferred to the SEC's Washington, D.C., office. I looked for a volunteer to keep the books, but wasn't able to find one. Rona had done bookkeeping years earlier, so we sent her to a class to learn Quick Books. I'm not a detail person, and I panicked over every mistake. It's important to avoid even the appearance of wrongdoing when we're representing God.

We keep the students foremost

When it looked as if we might not have the funding for the fall, 2001, class, Ron Arsenault offered to set up an endowment fund, and Keith Brisco started partnerships with prospective employers. Having people come to me with ideas rather than wait to be asked was encouraging.

As important as the business of Life Skills Lab was, it wasn't our reason for existing. Ministry is with people. No matter how well managed a program is, if you don't concentrate on outreach and services, if you didn't stay focused on the people you're serving, it is bound to fail.

With Phil teaching, Sabeldi in the computer lab, and Rona keeping books and helping in the office, we were in good shape for a staff. But we needed more money and referrals. We also needed to update our curriculum. The Adkins materials were great, but even the students noticed references to such jobs as typewriter repairman and charts with 19__ in the date column.

That summer, we concentrated on recruitment, visiting a dozen agencies, showing the excellent video Stan had produced, giving a brief talk, and leaving materials on Life Skills Lab. We notified the English, Spanish and Chinese congregations, and spoke and had a table at a Housing Agency Employment Fair. We sent releases to local newspapers and left flyers at check-cashing places and 99c stores.

We learn to work with the government

I had volunteered as one of the coordinators of an organization to plan the delivery of county services to families. That effort had paid off repeatedly through valuable contacts that helped our program. I attended the county-sponsored kick-off of an association of Faith-Based Organizations (fbo's) to see if any county funding was available.

I attended a county grantwriting workshop, and things looked promising for a Long-Term Family Self Sufficiency grant. The only snag was the length of our program. Our county supervisor, Yvonne Burke, sent her deputy to see if they could help us financially. He confirmed my fears that the county couldn't fund a training program that lasted as long as ours did. It seemed impossible to adequately prepare students for good jobs in less time, so we planned a proposal writing schedule and a benefit auction to raise money and prayed to be able to continue offering classes.

Our former assemblyman Kevin Murray was now a state senator. He was trying to get us into the 2001-02 state budget for a grant from the general fund. I had faxed him a copy of our generic proposal the previous year, but the legislature turned us down. I was thrilled that he hadn't forgotten us.

We wouldn't know the results until the budget passed that summer, and the money wouldn't come before October 1, after the fall class started. I prayed that we would get the grant and use it wisely.

Daniel is a model

The relationship between church and state has always been an uneasy one. We've looked at the lives and ministries of Nehemiah and Joseph, two believers who led urban redevelopment and food distribution projects while serving pagan governments. Another example is the prophet Daniel. Daniel and his three friends had been taken to Babylon in the first deportation of youthful hostages before the fall of Jerusalem (Daniel 1:3-20). These hostages were nobles—handsome, bright and well educated—hand-picked to serve the Babylonian king, Nebuchadnezzar.

Tensions rose when the young men refused to defile themselves with the king's food and wine. The Babylonians, like most Gentiles, ate foods forbidden by the Law of Moses and didn't keep kosher preparation rules. The official responsible for the young men was afraid they would not appear as healthy as those who ate the king's food. Daniel suggested a 10-day test on a diet of vegetables and water. At the end of the test, Daniel and his friends looked better nourished than the others.

God gave Daniel knowledge, including an understanding of dreams and visions. When the king tested him, he found him without equal. Then, in a situation reminiscent of Joseph's in Egypt, the Babylonian king had a dream (Daniel 2:1-48). His wise men and astrologers failed to interpret the dream because he refused to tell them what it was about. The king ordered his wise men, including Daniel, to be executed. Daniel prayed, and God revealed both the dream and its interpretation.

Daniel gave God the glory as he described the huge statue with a gold head, silver chest and arms, bronze belly and thighs, iron legs, and feet of iron mixed with clay. It was smashed by a rock into such small pieces that the wind swept them away. The statue represented a series of kingdoms beginning with the king's own, each inferior to the previous one. All were overcome by a kingdom that wouldn't be destroyed, the kingdom of God.

Daniel and his friends served the king, but they refused to do anything against God's will. Recognizing God's sovereignty over the kingdoms of men as well as over their own individual lives, they prayed for help to navigate the delicate balance between divine and human law. We needed to do the same.

Jesus articulated the principle in response to a question from the Pharisees: Were believers to pay taxes? Pointing to Caesar's portrait on a coin, Jesus said, "Give to Caesar what is Caesar's and to God what is God's" (Matthew 22:21). Peter and John emphasized half of the equation when they were warned not to teach in Jesus' name. "We must obey God rather than men!" they said (Acts 5:29). And Paul stressed the other side when he told Christians to submit "to the governing authorities, for there is no authority except that which God has established" (Romans 13:1).

We get needed help

That summer, my daughter Kathy, a school teacher, volunteered to help in the Life Skills Lab office. Unlike Rona and me, Kathy grew up with computers. She was a big help, particularly with the newsletter. Harding University students in Los Angeles for spring break helped as well. They planned an open house for prospective students, agencies, employers, and supporters. Lois Gomez, my fundraising teacher at UCLA, helped me start developing a strategy to sustain the program.

In July we received the call that answered our prayers. Life Skills Lab had been included in the budget of the State of California for a $100,000 grant! We had recruited students for a fall class, and now we would be able to pay for it. But even as our technical volunteer, Herman Roberts, searched for a good deal on computers to replace the used ones Bank of America had donated years earlier, it became obvious that the California economy was heading for a recession.

I work closely with government

Representatives of the state EDD came to Los Angeles to help us start the fund transfer process. There were conditions to fulfill and deadlines to meet, but contrary to some people's expectations, they didn't interfere with the church in any way. We had to keep records and make reports on the way we used the money and on the progress of the students. We had a lock installed on the file cabinet, and I was bonded to handle the funds. I was glad the state was careful about the way we used tax money.

Most of the grants administered by the EDD had gone to organizations with full staffs. None of us were even fulltime employees. We were understaffed for keeping all the required records. Also, we had been accepted for funding on the basis of a generic proposal written two years earlier. The budget did not reflect our current needs. We needed to rewrite the budget.

At first, I tried to do it myself, but I wasn't sure how to do it properly. Fortunately, the state had assigned us a program manager, Harnak Samra. I had been told that he was available for technical support, but I assumed that had to do with computers. It really meant he'd help us do what was needed to access the money the legislature had voted us. He talked me through the budget process, and we finished in a little over an hour. He explained that we'd make purchases, then submit receipts for reimbursement. Harnak was a Muslim, but he couldn't have worked harder for us if he had been a member at Culver Palms.

Lessons come from experience

One of the most important lessons I learned in working with the state was that they were just people with a job to do. If we were honest and treated them with respect, they gave us all the help we needed. We had an excellent relationship.

We wanted to use the money in ways that would strengthen the program for the long haul. In addition to operating expenses that directly served the students, we purchased ten new computers (giving us sixteen that could handle the current programs) and adjustable chairs for the computer room (replacing folding chairs with phone books for added height). We ordered updated curriculum as it became available, contracted with a local public relations firm to help get the program better known in the community and with a nonprofit consulting firm to do a financial analysis and fund development plan.

About that time, I began writing this urban ministry book. I was learning a great many things I felt might benefit others, and I wanted to get them down in a usable form. Things were moving and changing fast.

Thirty-six people—prospective students, graduates, volunteers, agency people, and supporters—attended our open house that August. The new curriculum arrived just before class began in September. Fourteen students were there the first day.

The next day was 9/11, and we dismissed early. I was concerned that the students might be afraid to come back, but only one failed to. One got a job a week later and left the class, and another got a great job a week or two before class ended. The remaining eleven students made up our largest graduating class ever.

In October, I had a tachycardia attack and spent three days in the hospital having tests. The cardiologist said I had to take it easier. I asked God to guide me as I paced and prioritized my work. I needed to overcome my fear of authority and let God help me do his will.

One of our graduates, Kim, had excellent computer skills and wanted to be an events planner. We hired her to work part-time in the office. Keesha got a job in a drug store while she studied for her beautician's license. Olivia studied to be an apartment manager. Jeff wanted to work as an armed security guard. Susan was interested in law. Carol got two jobs, with the YMCA and with law enforcement. Tanya attended West LA College to study accounting and ended up working there.

Margaret was our only Native American student. She was an artist, but after her husband left, she needed a more dependable income. She informed us when she enrolled that she had no interest in Bible study. We told her it wasn't required and were surprised when she was the only student who never missed a devotion. She has since become a member of the Agape fellowship. Margaret wanted to teach painting to children. When she injured her wrist, we helped her type the sample curriculum she'd developed for her interview. She was hired by Star Education to teach watercolor and pottery in a private and a public school. Yet another success.

The state funds are frozen

I was grateful that the grant came through just when we needed it, but it was a lot of work handling the business requirements while supervising and keeping records on our largest class ever. The grant was just for one year, but prospects looked good for continued state support. Harnak and others from Sacramento were impressed with our program. They used it as an example of best practices—particularly our mentoring program and our Graduate Seminar. An article about the seminar was printed in a publication for job training programs throughout the state. They were impressed with what we were able to accomplish with minimal money and staff. They knew programs like ours more than paid for themselves. By investing a limited, one-time sum to train a person to get work, the state saved years of welfare payments, established a pattern of family self-sufficiency, and increased the rolls of taxpayers.

But by late 2002, the state treasury was in trouble. I met with the people from Sacramento, and the message was clear. Between the energy crisis and the economic downturn, the state was running out of money.

Kathy and I listed everything in the checkbook, then crossed out everything we'd been reimbursed for. Everything that remained went into a final invoice. The state grant had been a short-lived but helpful influx of money. I wasn't sure we'd get all we requested in that invoice, but if we did, we'd have received over half the grant money in four months. Not bad under the circumstances.

I put together a new budget without the state funds, then sent out recruitment letters for the spring class. We addressed envelopes to our supporters list and enclosed the new publicity pieces the public relations firm had designed for us. That December, we received a check for $16,000 from the state, almost everything I'd requested. It had been a roller-coaster year, with a state grant won and lost, a faltering economy and high unemployment. It was the coldest December I could remember since we came to Los Angeles thirty-six years earlier.

Our grant is fully funded

Midway through January, Norma from the state office came to Los Angeles with news that our state grant had been reinstated. Concerned that we might have run out of cash, she had filled out an invoice for our basic expenses and brought the check with her. I was touched by her thoughtfulness and the effort she'd made to help us. It wasn't what we'd expected from a bureaucrat!

Like Daniel, we were able to work with the government while maintaining our Christian principles. I learned a number of lessons from the process:

- God can meet our needs—for money, experience, help and strength.
- Despite the importance of the business aspects of running a program, they can't be allowed to overshadow people.
- It is possible to walk that fine line between the things that are Caesar's and those that are God's.
- People won't reject you for holding onto your principles.
- Government isn't an enemy. It's just people, most of whom are eager to help good works.
- You may need to distinguish between matters of faith and matters of culture.
- Trust God.
- Write many thank you notes.
- Explore all the alternatives.
- Keep a record of what you learn.

God had a vision for our ministry, as well as for our city. Despite the fact that the year started badly and bad things happened before it ended, we received the funding and the students we needed, and our graduates were successful. I prayed that I would continue to trust God's vision, even when I couldn't see the way.

Questions for Discussion

1. How can we cope with difficult and even frightening people in our ministries?

2. What are the advantages and disadvantages of church/state cooperation?

3. How can we keep a ministry from becoming secondary to its business aspects?

4. How can we maintain the proper balance between what is Caesar's and what is God's?

5. Tell about a time when you were pleasantly surprised by kindness from an unexpected source. What did you learn when that happened?

CHAPTER 13

Working with Volunteers

Cuauhtemoc and Desiree Arieta are artists. Desiree was a Christian, but Cuauhtemoc wasn't, when I began using him for community outreach. But he was excellent at his craft, and a willing volunteer. I never worried about whether or not people had come to Christ before I put them to work. I felt that, the more involved they were with a variety of Christians, the more likely they were to meet someone who could lead them to Christ.

Dean Shaw, an effective evangelist, began studying with Cuauhtemoc. I was thrilled one night when Desiree called to invite me to join a group at the building and witness Cuauhtemoc's baptism, uniting him with Christ and them as a Christian couple.

Desiree and Cuauhtemoc had designed dramatic posters to advertise the "No to Violence" event that introduced the Life Skills Lab to the community. They were only two of about fifty volunteers who worked on that event. The members of the community outreach committee that had initially conceived the Life Skills Lab ministry were all volunteers. And literally hundreds of people volunteered to make the program a success.

Two questions arise in a program like Life Skills Lab: Can church ministries serve both the community and the church? And can the church and the community work together in ministry? Life Skills Lab was designed to serve both the community and the church. Needy people, both in and out of the church, were trained and encouraged to get jobs

and support their families through the program. And the ministry
offered an opportunity for people in what was essentially a middle-
class church to get involved in hands-on ministry to people in need.
After all, I began working with the Culver Palms Church in involvement
and outreach. Life Skills Lab was the single most effective ministry I
found to involve members of the church in serving those outside the
body. The second question, however, proved more complex. The
church and the community can work together in ministry, but the varied motivations and emphases of the two groups can threaten the success of the effort.

Most Christians worked with Life Skills Lab because, as children of
God and members of his family, the church, we are called to serve other
people. And we were seeking to glorify him by our efforts. But we
never turned down volunteers from the community, and often, when
we lacked people with the requisite skills, we actively sought the help
of non-Christians. I was most pleased when our students, both
Christians and non-Christians, volunteered to help in the classroom and
during special events.

Volunteers work together

Student growth and success were the greatest accomplishments of Life
Skills Lab. But our second greatest accomplishment was putting together an exceptional cadre of Christian servants to work together to help
them. We as Christians benefited almost as much as the students did
from the opportunities for service occasioned by the ministry. Whatever
our gifts—counseling, teaching, computer skills, giving, marketing, bookkeeping—we were able to glorify God by exercising those gifts to help
others. And the rewards were great.

Volunteers were the backbone of the program from the beginning.
Board members, mentors, office workers, counselors, special speakers,
and the staff of support services like the food pantry and the Back-to-
Work Boutique made the program work.

The volunteers with Life Skills Lab and other nonprofits who invest
the most in the programs are board members. They are responsible for
the fiscal success of the venture. For the first six years of the program,
the elders of the Culver Palms Church served as our board of directors.
They approved our plans to start the ministry in the first place, they

budgeted the church's contribution to it, and most of them participated as individuals, volunteering their time and expertise in various areas.

Tom Bost, the board secretary, offered the expertise of his law firm to shepherd our application through the complex process of nonprofit incorporation. Woody Hughes from Pepperdine's education faculty served as the first president of the board. Ron Lau, board treasurer, spoke to the students who came to Culver Palms as a part of the Mission Workshop at Pepperdine about the need for, and principles behind, Life Skills Lab. He also taught a weekly session on money management to help Life Skills Lab students use their money wisely once they got a job. Bernie James was a strong voice of support on the board as well as a personal advisor and encouragement to me. Dennis Lowe trained mentors. And Keith Brisco and Fred Ricker, who were deacons at the time but have since become elders, contributed to the ministry in a variety of ways.

New components address new needs

During the first class, we became aware that many of our students had been abused sexually. Jenny Ricker, a family counselor, volunteered to lead group counseling one afternoon a week to help them cope with this and other emotional problems that limited employability. Abused women have low self-esteem, and few things are more important in a job interview than a positive sense of self.

When we suspected that one of our students was abusing alcohol, Toby Considine added a recovery component to the program. Concerns about their children's progress in school led Melvia Jones, a junior high math teacher, to tutor the children and teach their mothers to work more effectively with them and their teachers.

Other volunteers helped in the computer lab and worked with our website. At one of our fundraisers, Dean Shaw talked about his joy at being able to use his professional training and experience as a software engineer to serve others through Life Skills Lab, combining his religious and professional life in a way he hadn't been able to in the past.

We learn about using volunteers

The Culver Palms Church was made up of people with a wide variety of talents that we were able to use for Life Skills Lab. Some of the lessons we learned in the process were the following:

1. Using volunteers demands flexibility. Gail Brisco, a working mother on disability leave from her company, put together a three-part curriculum that she taught as her health permitted. Sometimes she didn't know until the day of the class if she'd be able to come, but the students always benefited from her presentations. Another volunteer offered a resume writing workshop for each class by taking two mornings off her job.

2. Take advantage of special areas of expertise. Carla Williams, who owns a job placement agency, talked with the students about their career plans and the job market and conditions in their chosen fields. Char Dolton, who interviews for Jet Propulsion Laboratory, conducted mock interviews with members of each class. The interviews were taped and played back, and Char critiqued the student's efforts.

Willia Osby, who had put together outfits for celebrities at Saks Fifth Avenue, put together outfits for our students as well. One of the students told the advisory board that, before she came to Life Skills Lab, she didn't know you weren't supposed to wear jeans and a T-shirt for a job interview.

3. Let the volunteer set the limits. Some volunteers may want to do something totally different from their professional lives. My daughter Kathy taught high school kids all week. When she got a break, she was not eager to work with teens or teach, but she enjoyed the creative work of designing a newsletter.

Mentors are basic

Mentors were a key component of Life Skills Lab from the beginning. Members of the congregation were matched with students to befriend and encourage. Mentors were advocates for one particular student, and committed to a contact a week by phone, card or visit.

We put together a mentor training pamphlet based on parts of the HUD mentoring program and held training sessions led by a family counselor and a pediatrician.

About thirty different members of the Culver Palms church served as mentors for at least one class during the six years classes were offered. Keith Brisco mentored students in almost every class. Cathy Somar was an excellent and devoted mentor, and Dean and Kelly Shaw took turns mentoring.

Mentors befriended the students—inviting them into their homes, visiting the students' homes, studying with and praying for them, and inviting them to worship. Again, the key is flexibility. Some mentors worked with a student's entire family, while others worked with their student alone. Some made a special effort to help their student find information on such areas as low-cost beautician training or transferring nursing experience from another country to the United States.

Support services address student needs

The fact that our students didn't have jobs often meant that they were short of cash for other basic needs as well. The church's food pantry was available for students who needed groceries. The Back-to-Work Boutique, a clothes closet filled with used clothing suitable for interviews, was popular. Each student got as many outfits as she could wear, and all the students, from the smallest to the largest, got something.

Many of our students didn't have cars, and others had old cars that broke down frequently, so one group of volunteers kept us supplied with bus tokens. Others made cash donations to help keep the program afloat.

College students volunteer

Students and faculty members from Pepperdine University volunteered in various ways. Students in business classes prepared needs analyses, marketing plans and budgets that gave them experience and provided us with free consulting services. Other classes, as well as individual students, helped organize the food pantry, sort clothing for the Back-to-Work Boutique, and connect us to the Internet. They wrote encouraging notes to students and turned orange from eating carrots in a novel fundraising drive!

Groups of students from Christian colleges in other states spent their spring breaks serving in urban ministries, both at the church building and in other parts of the city. It was a lot of work to prepare for these groups and organize their activities while they were here, but they always infused us with energy, enthusiasm, and new ideas. We hoped that some would become interested in working in Los Angeles, and in 2003, we were thrilled when Jason and Leah Tomlinson, who had come for two years as Harding students, became the first students to move here to do urban ministry.

Community people participate

Personnel from the schools and agencies that referred students to Life Skills Lab were valued partners in our work. Local physicians and a public health nurse taught sessions on preventive medicine which helped our students remain in class and avoid costly care. Career counselors from local job-placement agencies, both public and private, made helpful presentations.

Local restaurateur Jay Handel made a generous contribution of space, food and staff for fundraising events. Special events are popular because they involve a large number of volunteers and generate publicity and good will. The problem with events is that it's easy to spend more money than you bring in.

Our first events were benefit brunches held each December at Jay's San Gennaro restaurant. At first, we paid a reduced rate for the food, but before long, all proceeds went to Life Skills Lab. Ticket sales for the first brunch, after the first class graduated in 1997, totaled three thousand dollars.

In June of 2001, we held our first benefit auction. We solicited items from local businesses and individuals to offer in live and silent auction segments. Marla Lombard, a member of my writing group who had worked for Christie's Auction House in New York, served as auctioneer. My doctor donated tongue depressors, and volunteers from Pepperdine's human resources department made paddles and helped photograph the items for the auction book. Our son Robert, in a black suit and white gloves, showed the items up for auction. The support of my family and friends was consistently gratifying.

A local frame company and an antique store donated reproductions. We had tickets to a sports event and a drama presentation, as well as certificates from restaurants, a health spa, a hairdresser, and a hotel. Items from individuals included original art and time and skills—to give a massage, entertain children, and help organize a wardrobe.

Thirty people attended, and we cleared $2,000. It was the largest number of thank-you notes I'd written since the program began.

Body language

The Apostle Paul, in various of his epistles, refers to the church as a body. We are the body of Christ. Different parts of the church have different functions, just as different parts of the human body. God has gifted his people to fulfill those various functions, and none of us should exalt ourselves or look down on others because our gifts differ. (See 1 Corinthians 12:12-27).

Because God has given us gifts—and the greatest gift of all, our life in Jesus Christ—we respond by reaching out in loving service to those around us. Robert Kolb gives the following five responses of the body to the grace of God in Jesus Christ:[1]

1. Faith recognizes that God is a good and loving God.

2. The believer acknowledges God's goodness in his restoring righteousness through his Word, in the flesh, in forgiveness, and through communion with him and with each other.

3. God's gift in Jesus elicits a trust in him that allows us to risk what he has given us in our efforts to carry his love to others.

4. God's gift of Christ's righteousness means that believers are willing to submit to him for the sake of the neighbor's need.

5. Christians enjoy doing the work of God because they realize that it gives witness to God's love and forms an important part of their testimony to the Father who has reclaimed and recreated them.

Questions for Discussion

1. Should the church serve both Christians and non-Christians? What are some arguments for and against?

2. What about using volunteers from both groups? Again, what could the advantages and drawbacks be?

3. How is the church, when its members work together in ministry, like a human body?

4. What attitudes can get in the way of the harmonious function of the body?

5. What are some of the advantages and pitfalls of special events?

CHAPTER 14

The End of Life Skills Lab

It was the fall of 2002, and our second fundraising auction was well underway. Brotman Hospital, across the street from the church building, had donated the use of their auditorium, a lovely venue housed in a historic mission-style building with a two-story entry area and a sweeping wrought-iron and tile stairway to the auditorium area on the second floor.

Earlier that year, the elders had decided to turn over fiduciary responsibilities to the group that had served as our advisory board. That group had been actively involved in the program since they began doing evaluation early in the program's history, and I felt they would make an excellent board of directors.

The new board had worked hard over the summer to plan and carry out the auction, and their efforts were obvious. The event was beautiful. The two-story entry area was filled with colorful kites, a symbol of the hope Life Skills Lab gave its students. In addition to the board and family and friends, we were joined by volunteers from West Los Angeles College and Disney VoluntEARS.

Board members had taken responsibility for various tasks for the auction. Joan handled printing and mailing invitations, Jay provided food, Jennine arranged for a live band, Jennie and I solicited donations from local business, Susan sold tickets and handled the money, and Ruben worked on set-up and arranged for the donation of a painting by a well-known local artist.

Our local city councilman had the auction book printed, an upscale furniture store contributed a club chair and a $1,000 gift certificate, and Debbie Allen offered free lessons at her dance studio. Church members donated their skills at everything from detailing an automobile to cooking a romantic French dinner.

Conflict arose when some members of the board wanted a casino night in addition to the auction. Some church people didn't approve. Of course, a casino night fundraiser isn't actually gambling. No one wins any money, as all the proceeds go to the charity. By this time, Life Skills Lab was no longer receiving financial support from the church. I asked God's guidance as we walked that fine line between the sacred and the secular.

Community people had made financial contributions and helped with fundraising to support the program since it began. Dick Pancost had served on the advisory board and helped with grant writing. Others worked on special events and contributed items and services for the first auction. A number of the new board members were community people. They were responsible for the work now, and they made the decisions. Those attending had fun and spent money. Although attendance was small, we took in $8,000, clearing $6,000 after expenses. It was our most profitable fundraiser ever.

Money is tight

The state grant initially was for just one year, and it had already funded classes in the fall of 2001 and the spring of 2002. Fortunately, the state had given us an extension until December, which allowed us to offer a third class in the fall of 2002. During the time the grant was in effect, we had brought in enough money through our own fundraising efforts to pay for a fourth class in the spring of 2003. While we had the grant, reporting demands were great, and I wasn't able to do as much fundraising as I'd hoped, but I felt confident that the grant would be renewed.

The bad economy was hurting everyone. We sent proposals to several private foundations without success. I worked on yet another proposal for California Community Foundation, and one of their program managers visited our facilities. It was the third proposal I'd written them, but we wouldn't know their response until September. I met with Santa Monica College and Catholic Charities to explore partnering on a Compassion

Capital grant from the federal government. We were too small to apply on our own.

At a Faith-Based Economic Summit where corporate funders, private foundations and government funders spoke, the grants manager for Wells Fargo all but promised a $10,000 donation to job training programs that applied. With the $20,000 we had left over, it could fund another class in the fall of 2003. Brian Brookey wrote the application, and the grants manager sent us a check for $1,000, together with an apologetic note. They had spent all the funds allotted for contributions and had nothing left to give.

We sent direct mail letters to the members of the West Los Angeles and Culver City Chambers of Commerce as well as the church. That brought in some money, but not enough. Our individual supporters were suffering from the bad economy as well.

The business people on the board were appalled by our lack of reserves. Except for the period of the state grant, we had operated on faith—raising funds for one class at a time. The money we needed had always come in before the next class began. It made absolutely no sense to business people.

Based on my training in fundraising and our fund development plan, I suggested a major gifts campaign. Giving and soliciting donations are primary responsibilities of a nonprofit board. If each member gave $1,000 and solicited similar contributions from five of their friends, we could fund classes for a year and buy the time to develop better alternatives. I gave my $1,000 and began soliciting donations from people I knew.

Instead, the board hired a grantwriter for half of the money we had left. She applied to some foundations that didn't fund job training, some that funded training for teens but not adults, and some that didn't fund in our geographic area. Of course, any money she raised wouldn't have come in time to pay for a class in the fall. Foundations don't respond that quickly.

We disagree on roles

When the elders had served as the board of Life Skills Lab, I reported to them and they let me know what they wanted from me in regular monthly meetings. But they pretty well left day-to-day operations to me.

The new board was much more hands-on, and at first I was grateful. It was wonderful to feel that others were taking a part of the load. But it was also hard to find my place in what had suddenly become a ministry with a dozen heads, all seeming to want different things.

Some of their plans involved spending money we didn't have—often at little return that I could see. The previous November, a new member of the church, Merie Fregia, had stopped by to help with our website. A student at California State University Los Angeles, she knew a lot about computers, marketing, and graphics. I hired her on the spot—just part time and at very low pay—to take the place of Kim, the graduate who had quit that summer. Merie was helping put together a newsletter to inform supporters of our needs.

The board questioned my hiring Merie without consulting them, even though at the time they were still functioning as an advisory board. They wanted us to rewrite the newsletter and add a section that essentially was an advertisement.

They insisted on a new phone line so the phone wouldn't be answered by the church, which was providing the service for free. It had never seemed to hurt us in the past, but one board member was sure her friends would be turned off by any connection with a church. We spent money we didn't have to buy a phone, pay for the service, and have our business cards and letterheads reprinted with the new number. Meanwhile, the church gave our old number to the Chinese minister. We didn't know until later that he hadn't been picking up his messages. We'd had many calls from people who must have been bewildered to hear a message in Chinese!

The board wanted a new needs assessment. I felt we could get by with the old one until we were more stable financially, but Merie and I began collecting the data. We created endless spreadsheets. We gathered census figures, called our thirty referral agencies to determine how many students they might send, and contacted other organizations doing job training in the area for information on the services they provided. Several wanted to send students to us because we had a more intensive program.

Phil wasn't planning to return in the fall. At graduation in April, we honored him for his outstanding work as Life Skills Lab instructor, and I began looking for someone who might take his place.

We disagree philosophically

There were areas where the board and I disagreed philosophically. For instance, some members suggested that, since there was no demand for employees in the sagging economy, there didn't seem to be any need to train people to get jobs. I felt the need was greater than ever. There always are jobs. Even in the worst of times, people get work. Our students had been taught a lot of ways to find jobs, and they had lower expectations than many people in the job market. They were motivated enough to take what they could get and work up from there. The question boiled down to a basic one of purpose: Were we there to serve employers, or families that needed help?

When the minister told me the church would need my office by the summer of 2003, I prayed that we would be able to find new office space. I felt caught between outsiders who didn't appreciate our religious emphasis and Christians who didn't want the program to be a drain on the church. I just wanted it to survive. It seemed to be doing a lot of good. If the outsiders didn't like the Christian emphasis, they should pay the expenses themselves. If they expected the church to support the program, they should be satisfied with the way we did it.

I fail to make the case

Good communications between the executive director and the board are basic to the sound operation of a corporation, but our board was growing increasingly hostile, and I was increasingly fearful, dreading to see them. They made demands, and I got defensive. They blamed me and I blamed them. I didn't understand all that was happening, but I knew it wasn't good.

I believed God had given me a work to do for him on the Westside of Los Angeles. When things started going wrong, I just dug my heels in deeper. Prayed harder. Worked harder. It had always been effective before. Despite the fact that I prided myself on being innovative and exploring all the options, I really was pretty conservative. I wasn't inclined to totally rethink the concept.

I didn't want to believe that the difficulties might be God's will. I forgot that it all depended on him and felt that it all depended on me. I forgot that, if God saw fit for Life Skills Lab to end, it would, despite my best efforts. And by that point, I was too stressed to give it my best efforts. I was short with people and pinched and running scared.

Other problems contributed

Other problems contributing to the end of Life Skills Lab include the following:

1. *Churches of Christ traditionally haven't emphasized social work.* We seem to have confused social efforts with the social gospel. The gospel of Jesus is his death, burial and resurrection. That's what saves us. Not anything we do. However, we're still supposed to do good, show compassion and serve others out of love and gratitude.

2. *We have a tendency toward trends.* In many of our churches, one thing is big for a while, then it dies and another becomes the emphasis. Work with those in need demands steady commitment and long-term investment. We need consistency and persistence.

3. *Most of our money goes for the local work.* Most of our budgets are spent within the walls of our buildings—for preachers' salaries, building upkeep, and education programs, with little left for benevolence and evangelism. It seems the reverse of Jesus' emphasis.

4. *Ministries must remain focused on their mission.* We can't let personal aggrandizement, favors for friends, or any other lesser goals take preeminence. Politics can creep into even the best of efforts. People can do good work for bad motives.

5. *Board training is essential.* Volunteers need to understand the responsibilities of a nonprofit board, including giving and soliciting donations. A weekend training session just after the new board took over could have gotten us started on the same page and avoided misunderstandings.

It all depends on me

Despite the fact that God had blessed our efforts beyond anything I could have imagined and that a large group of Christians and non-Christians were working together to make the program a success, on some level I still felt that it all depended on me. Part of it was the "buck stops here" responsibility of any leader. But another part was a failure of leadership. Sometimes I failed to delegate, and sometimes, when I did turn a responsibility over to someone else, I failed to let him or her accept responsibility if it didn't work out. If it looked as if a job wasn't getting done, I'd jump in and do it myself.

Harold Shank, in his book *Loosening Your Grip*, refers to the "five words that keep us from seeing the difference between being dependable and being indispensable, that blind us to the discrepancy between *irresponsible* and *irreplaceable*. It's a faulty belief that pushes us into overdrive when we should be in park, that destroys our spirit when we should be restoring our soul. It all depends on me."

He calls that brief sentence "the whopper" that "makes me view all of life as something *I* do. Life becomes making a list and checking off each completed task. As I increasingly distrust others to accomplish their assigned tasks, I become more convinced that I should trust only myself."[1]

As Harold points out, self-sufficiency is the ploy the Devil used against Jesus (Matthew 4:1-11)—the temptation to feel that he had to take matters into his own hands, to build his own kingdom, to test his own security system. "The devil's words boil down to one thing: Be in control. Don't trust God to control your life. Control it yourself. It all depends on you."

But "Jesus trusted God," Harold says. "He trusted God with his life. Forty days without food, but God will provide. He trusted God with his kingdom. Thirty years old and no following at all, but God will provide. He trusted God with his future. Three years until he died in Jerusalem, but Jesus knew God would provide."[2]

At my best, I knew it, too. But I wasn't always at my best.

A painful blow

Just before the regular meeting of the board in May of 2003, as I was assembling the data they had requested for the needs assessment, three members came in and asked me to resign. I was stunned. They told me I could stay for the meeting and that I'd have until the first of the month to clear out my office. They would pay my salary through June. I offered to supply information—on prospective students, the steps to take to prepare for the next class, and where things were located in the office— if they wanted to continue offering classes. But I was afraid it meant the end of Life Skills Lab.

I was deeply disappointed and discouraged. Though Life Skills Lab was the most difficult work I had ever done, it also was the most satisfying. It was hard to lose a job at my age in a difficult job market. I sympathized in a way I hadn't been able to before with our unemployed students. More of my self-worth than I'd realized had been tied up in my work.

Though the board did not make a formal announcement until months later, it soon became apparent that not just my job, but the whole program, was ending. It hurt to think that desperate people wouldn't have access to the training that had brought hope and help to so many.

Life Skills Lab was worth the effort

I have no regrets about the time and effort I put into Life Skills Lab. During the life of the program, we offered ten classes—one a year in 1997, '98, and '99; two a year in 2000, '01, and '02; and a final class in 2003. Sixty-seven students graduated from those classes, not counting those who got jobs just before their classes ended. That's over 70 families with a breadwinner trained to get and keep a job.

Most of our students have done just that, some with remarkable success. Over 70 precious individuals have developed self-confidence, learned to get and keep a job, gained skills, and better realized their potential to be independent, contributing members of society. We introduced them to God and encouraged them to develop a relationship with him.

I learned a lot from my experience with Life Skills Lab—program development, fundraising, finances, computer skills, volunteer management, networking, recruitment. And I was always able to find excellent volunteers to supply what I didn't know. I learned about myself—that I had talents I never would have suspected, that I'm more of a control freak than I realized, and that I wasn't always the communicator I thought I was. I made many mistakes, but they were mistakes of judgment, not intent. Mostly, I learned to trust God and not feel so indispensable.

The following are some of the lessons of Life Skills Lab:

1. God is in control—not me. He won't necessarily give me what I want, even if I pray fervently for it.

2. Different people have different values and aims. No matter how hard I tried to put together the best program I knew how, others—even those in authority—would disagree with my judgment. I could insist on my own vision, but if I did, I had to be prepared to take the consequences.

3. Resources are required for any large project—resources of personnel, money, supporters, technical skills, and good will.

4. When some people are faced with a problem, they'll ask for a spreadsheet.

5. Be honest and upright in all your dealings. You may not be able to convince everyone, but at least you can live with yourself.

6. Be humble. Always be willing to admit what you don't know. Someone will know and be willing to teach you.

7. Be focused. Whatever your ministry, concentrate first on the people you're trying to help.

8. You can't do your best on everything. Learn to distinguish between the tasks that demand your best and those that just need to get done.

9. Maintain the personal touch.

10. Don't be discouraged. You won't always win. Don't be afraid to try again.

Accepting God's will

Sometimes it isn't so much a matter of catching God's vision as accepting his will. I had envisioned Life Skills Lab serving people in the area for decades to come. I had envisioned myself leading it as long as I had the strength. I had envisioned training someone like Merie to take over when I left. But my vision wasn't God's. Maybe because of my faults and failings. Maybe because of tensions inherent in the situation— church vs. state, sacred vs. secular, idealistic vs. pragmatic. Maybe because of conflicting personalities or visions. Maybe because God was ready to use me in other ways. Whatever the reason, the result was the same. I had to bring my vision more into alignment with his. I had to stop wanting things my way, stop kicking against the pricks. I had to accept God's will and trust him to know what was best.

Had I missed the point? I don't think so. Was this ministry God's will? I believe it was. Life Skills Lab did—and continues to do—a lot of good. God blessed it through eight years of planning and offering classes. He blessed us with over 70 precious people, most of whom made extraordinary changes in their lives. He blessed us with a small army of volunteers who worked together, demonstrating the model of the church as a body composed of different members with different functions, working together for a common goal.

That has to be a big part of God's vision for urban ministry.

Questions for Discussion

1. What are some circumstances beyond our control that can damage a ministry?

2. What attitudes and behaviors of ours can contribute to its demise?

3. Name three essentials of a good relationship between the administrators of a program and its board of directors.

4. What are some lessons we can learn about ministry from the fact that a particular work may not continue?

5. Is there a difference between being faithful and being successful? What is it?

CHAPTER 15

God's Vision
for Urban Ministry

God has a vision for his children in the city. He has a vision for you, and he has a vision for me. Though his plans for my life are different from what I once thought, that doesn't mean they're any less legitimate. He is the Lord of my life. He is in control. He can take me out of one ministry and put me into another whenever he chooses, as he has repeatedly during my forty years in Los Angeles.

He still wants me to do good, wherever I am, in whatever way I can. He wants me to serve him and other people, and he wants me to serve here in Los Angeles. I know that because this is where I am. When we first came to Los Angeles in the 60s, a popular poster read, "Bloom where you're planted." He's planted me here, and he expects me to continue faithfully to spread the fragrance of his love in this place.

He wants you to do the same. How can you discover and carry out your ministry? Glance over the following topics, and jot down two or three of the numbered sections that you would like to concentrate on. They should be topics of special interest or relevance to you and/or your ministry.

1. Listen and respond to God's call.

Has God called you to the city? to a particular ministry there? Does your heart ache for the needs of people in the city? youth? the homeless? single moms? the troubled? the lost?

First, obey God's general call, answer his invitation to relationship with him. Be baptized and put away your old life of sin and selfishness. Put on a new life of holiness and concern for others.

Get to know and love the city. See where he's already put you, and serve there first—in your family, among your neighbors, on your job, and in your local congregation. Find a small part of the city that you can touch. Take on some task that will bring your city closer to God's vision for it.

Then, pray that he'll lead you to a specific call, a place where he wants you to serve him. God has prepared a city for us. We begin to experience it as we answer his call and give ourselves to his control.

2. Communicate God's love.

Learn to communicate God's love, even to those who don't speak the same language you do. Study the cultures in your area—either formally in classes or informally through experience, reading and observation. Make friends of people from other cultures. Appreciate the variety of people in the city, their varied gifts and strengths.

Adjust personally and help your congregation adjust as a body to changes in neighborhood demographics. Be hospitable to immigrants moving into your area. Practice at home what we've sent missionaries abroad to do.

Cultural differences can be opportunities for greater understanding. Don't be afraid to ask about practices and attitudes you don't understand. Different doesn't necessarily mean wrong. Be alert to the differences among people of the same ethnic group based on varied levels of assimilation and socioeconomics.

3. Help those in need.

You can't solve all the problems of poverty, but you can share food, clothing, education or health care with those in need. Programs that help others to help themselves can make a long-term difference.

As you give to those in need, learn to receive with gratitude and grace. Don't fall for advertising that appeals to selfish desires. If you handle your own resources wisely, you'll have more to share with others.

Don't assume that people don't want to change. Most do, often they just don't know how. You can help the homeless or help prevent homelessness. You can give money or teach people to earn and use money wisely. You can help the mentally ill and addicted to recover, help the working poor make salaries that provide at least the basics for their families, donate school supplies, or volunteer with schools in disadvantaged areas.

4. Fight crime and violence.

Jesus taught us to turn the other cheek and treat others with respect and concern. We are our brothers' keepers, responsible for their safety and welfare.

We can start by promoting peace in our families and workplaces, being willing for others to have more than we do, and keeping competition within bounds.

Young people need viable alternatives to violence, including time from an interested adult. Spending an hour a week tutoring or mentoring a young person can make a big difference in his future.

5. Consider your role in the church.

Does your definition of church involve people outside the building? Consider your role in the church as serving rather than being served. Be outward-looking, not in-turned, and encourage your congregation to do the same.

Promote fellowship, but not at the expense of others. Make more non-Christian friends. Reach out to others, and involve them in your activities. Encourage other Christians to use their gifts to serve outsiders.

Relate to your community as Jesus did, by being in the world but not of it. Identify with others while retaining your identity as God's child.

6. Build bridges.

Are you a bridge builder, building bridges between the church and the city? Do you recognize the need all people have for Christ? Can you devise strategies to bring them together?

Help the church in your community to be known for doing positive things. Promote the strengths of other Christians. Be present in the world to listen to, identify with, and serve others.

Study the Bible, your faith community and your urban context to bridge effectively among them. Teach and live scripture, encourage the gifts of fellow church members to reach out and serve, and help develop creative programs to reach your city.

7. Be like Jesus.

Jesus initiated our relationship with him by seeking us out. We can seek out others. He shared our experience. We can empathize with others. He touched the hurting, met needs, and entered into relationship with those around him. He called sinners and served them. We can do the same.

Give God room to work. Work and invest to change lives rather than just meet needs. Emphasize relationships.

See what other churches are doing. Study their most effective practices, and incorporate those that fit your context.

8. Pray constantly.

Pray, expecting God's guidance and intervention. Be alert to the wonders he scatters on our paths. Trust him for wisdom and strength. Network and plan with prayer. Seek his will, not his buy-in to your plan. Ask him for all your needs, large and small. Pray with faith that God will provide. Rely on him, not on yourself.

See what God has done, and thank him for answered prayer.

9. Learn how to serve.

Don't let the immediate needs of those you serve distract you from their deeper needs. But recognize that you may have to address immediate needs before people will share their deeper ones. Go for long-term solutions, not just quick fixes.

Be flexible. There are no hard and fast rules in dealing with people. Be creative. Come up with original ways to help. There are no "one-size-fits-all" solutions. If you can't help, find someone who can. Take advantage of local resources. If you don't know the person or answer you need, spread the word. Someone will know.

As much as possible, serve the whole person—body, mind, emotions and spirit. Celebrate successes.

Take advantages of opportunities to learn, grow and develop in your ministry. Get training. Enlist volunteers. Appreciate differences in personality, style, and strengths. Part of God's plan is that his people work together, benefiting from their differences.

10. Sustain your ministry.

Give first, then ask others to give. Accept all gifts graciously—money, time, and talents. Be generous with what you have, and expect others to do the same. Generosity is a Christian virtue.

Seek help with fundraising. Put together a generic proposal, then adapt it to specific funders. Follow guidelines precisely. Clarify your goals and how you'll determine when you've met them. Plan how you'll implement objectives. Describe vividly what you do to meet needs. Use examples.

Approach prospective funders from their perspective. How can you help them achieve their aims? How can you assure them that you can do what you say you will?

Expect negative responses to grant proposals. Only about one in ten are funded. Check with funders who have rejected your requests to see how you can do better next time.

11. Maintain Balance.

How can you maintain balance between your personal and professional life? Successes and failures? Dreams and reality?

Recognize the difference between your responsibility and God's. God is in control. Seek his direction. Accept help and learn how to use it effectively. Many people will help if you let them know how they can. Take advantage of your contacts. You never know who God can use for his purposes. Don't hesitate to ask.

No one is indispensable—not even you. Accept responsibility for your part in problems, but don't always blame yourself. Evaluate yourself and your motives and methods, but focus on success. Concentrate on the good things that are happening—the people helped, the lives changed by your ministry. Look for God's hand and praise him for it. Don't lose track of the important things.

12. Learn to work with government.

Explore resources at all levels of government—city, county, state and federal. Don't depend on any single source for funding. Seek out experts on church/state issues

Keep good records, both financial and service.

Keep those you serve foremost. Don't neglect the program for the details of business and reporting.

13. Learn to work with volunteers.

Value all your volunteers. Utilize the resources of church, university, and community.

Establish good one-on-one relationships with your board. Express your appreciation for their contributions. Find training to help your board understand and fulfill their responsibilities. Clarify roles and responsibilities. Clarify the mission of the organization, and focus on it. Communicate clearly and openly. Don't get defensive.

Circumstances can conspire to destroy any program. Don't ignore God's part in those circumstances. If a ministry ends, concentrate on the good it's done and the lessons you've learned. Continue to do the good you can.

As God's children in the city, let's catch his vision for ministry and service and be Christ's body, touching the needs of his world.

Learning To Let Go

As Christians, we experience opposing forces—beginnings and endings, joy and sorrow, tension and release. I've been through a period of tension—of working, probably longer and harder than I should have, to keep a ministry going that God and other people decided had served its purpose. Now it's time to relax and see what he has in store.

Isaiah tells us that

Those who wait on the Lord
Shall renew their strength;
They shall mount up with wings like eagles,
They shall run and not be weary,
They shall walk and not faint.

I'm a workaholic. Work is easy for me. It's the waiting that's hard. I find it easier to *do* than to *be*. Since Life Skills Lab ended, I've enjoyed spending more time with my family, reflecting on my ministry, catching up with friends, and learning to wait on the Lord. I'm feeling the joy and strength seep back into my soul and spirit.

I'm happiest when I'm giving of myself to help others, but that is not all God has for me to do. He has given me a family and friends, and he wants me to enjoy them. He has given me health, and he wants me to take better care of it. He has given me a gift for writing, and he expects me to use it. Life Skills Lab became all-consuming. I'm enjoying having a job now that I can come home from and do some of the other things God has for me to do.

When Life Skills Lab ended, someone asked me if I was planning to leave the Culver Palms Church. I was surprised they'd even ask. Culver Palms is my neighborhood church. I have friends here. There is no other church in the city I'd rather worship with. It's not perfect, but neither am I. We need to keep working and serving together to find and do God's will more completely.

When the Holy Spirit filled the apostles on the day of Pentecost, they went out into the world to spread the good news of God's love expressed in Jesus. But they started in Jerusalem—right where they were, in their own community. That is the challenge—to spread the good news where we live, work and go to school.

There are times in our lives as God's children in the city when we feel as dead as Lazarus, when the color, life and beauty of our faith has faded, and we feel spiritually drained. But God keeps his promises. He provides for his children. And he calls us daily to "come forth" from the grave of disappointment and discouragement to a new life of service and dedication. Faith isn't irrelevant. So long as we trust God and work with him to make things better, he takes care of us, reviving our spirits and strength.

I'm learning not to be afraid. Fear is the opposite of faith. I'm learning to pray more, and less selfishly, and less often with my own agenda in mind. I need to be more open to God's direction. I need to let go of Life Skills Lab while not forgetting its lessons. I need to accept the inevitable failures and successes of life and wait on the Lord.

God loves this city and all cities, because they are his. He has a vision for the city and its people. He has a vision for us, his people in the city. And he has a vision for me. I pray that I'll catch that vision and continue to be his child in Los Angeles—in his time and in his way.

I can't meet all the needs of the city, even all the needs of those people I come in contact with. But I'm grateful that God has allowed me to work with him and others in helping those we have helped in the past and reaching out to others in the future.

At worship recently, one of our elders read a letter from the chairman of the board of Life Skills Lab. In it, he explained that the program had ended because of a lack of funds. That certainly was one reason. It also ended because of a lack of vision. We caught it for a moment—the vision of serving God by serving single mothers on the Westside of Los Angeles, the vision of working together, guided by his Spirit. We worked with him and for him, we glorified him and helped many people who glorified him as well. But that vision flickered and dimmed. It died for a moment in that place at that time, but it will spring back to life again here and in other places, now and at other times, in cities great and small all over the world.

God sees so much further than we do. He sees the potential of the cities we live in and the people we meet. He sees my potential as his child in this city. He wants others to glorify him because of the good I do. He wants my light to join with the lights of other Christians in this city and other cities around the globe and multiply into a blaze of light and praise and glory.

NOTES

Chapter One

1. Os Guinness, *The Call: Finding and Fulfilling the Central Purpose of Your Life* (Nashville, TN: Word, 1998), 24.

2. "Urban Population Continues to Grow," Penn State website, www.ems.psu.edu/info/explore/Urban Pop.html, 8/10/01.

3. *Los Angeles Times*, Friday, March 30, 2001, 1.

4. Naomi H. Rosenblatt and Joshua Horwitz, *Wrestling with Angels: What Genesis Teaches Us about Our Spiritual Identity, Sexuality, and Personal Relationships* (New York: Bantam Doubleday Dell Publishing Group, Inc., 1995), 93-101.

5. Guinness, *The Call*, 4.

6. Rosenblatt, *Wrestling with Angels*, 100.

7. Robert C. Linthicum, *City of God/City of Satan: A Biblical Theology of the Urban Church* (Grand Rapids, MI: Zondervan, 1991), 36.

Chapter Two

1. Milton Jones, *Christ—No More, No Less: How to Be a Christian in a Postmodern World* (Orange, California: New Leaf Books, 2001), 141-2.

2. Jones, 142-3.

3. Nina Weinstein, *Whaddaya Do?* (Old Tappan, NJ: ELS Educational Services, 1982).

4. Lucile Todd, "God Willing," *Trusting Women: The Way of Women in Churches of Christ*, Billie Silvey, editor (Orange, California: New Leaf Books, 2002), 208.

5. Calvin H. Bowers, *Realizing the California Dream: The Story of the Black Churches of Christ in Los Angeles* (2001), 149-50.

6. Ray Bakke with Jim Hart, *The Urban Christian: Effective Ministry in Today's Urban World* (Downers Grove, Illinois: InterVarsity, 1987), 136.

7. Bakke, 133.

8. Bakke, 139.

Chapter Three

1. *Keeping Our Promise: Strategic Planning Process, 1998-2003*, a publication of

the YMCA of Metropolitan Los Angeles, November 4, 1997.

2. United Way of Greater Los Angeles: Strategic Action Plan, adopted June 18, 1992, 4.

3. Linthicum, *Empowering the Poor: Community Organizing among the City's 'Rag, Tag, and Bobtail* (Monrovia, CA: MARC, 1991), 107.

4. Linthicum, 35.

5. Ronald J. Sider, *Rich Christians in an Age of Hunger: Moving from Affluence to Generosity* (Dallas: Word, 1997, 44-45.

6. PATH Conference on Poverty and Homelessness, Los Angeles: People Assisting the Homeless, July 10, 2002.

7. Dickerson, Marla, "State's Poverty Profile Changes," *Los Angeles Times*, August 26, 2002, 1.

8. Sider, *Rich Christians*, 89.

Chapter Four

1. Rick Marrs, *Embracing the Call of God: Finding Ourselves in Genesis* (Webb City, MO: Covenant Publishing, 2003), 75.

2. *Wrestling with God*, 57.

3. Ibid., 54-5.

4. Ibid., 59.

Chapter Five

1. J. Timothy Kauffman, "Structures, injustice, and insensitivity: Who is the neighbor, anyway?" *God So Loves the City: Seeking a Theology for Urban Mission*, Charles Van Engen and Jude Tiersma, editors (Monrovia, CA: MARC, 1994), 40.

2. Richard Gollings, "Planting covenant communities of faith in the city," *God So Loves*, 134.

3. Ibid., 135.

4. C. Leonard Allen, *Distant Voices: Discovering a Forgotten Past for a Changing Church* (Abilene, TX: ACU Press, 1993), 92.

5. Ibid., 94.

6. Harold Shank, Anthony Wood, and Ron Bergeron, *Up Close and Personal: Embracing the Poor* (Joplin, MO: College Press, 2000), 88.

7. Harold Shank, "Nashville's Central Church of Christ," *Restoration Quarterly*, 41.1 (1999), 19.

8. Ibid., 23-24.

9. Jimmie Moore Mankin, "The Role of Social Service in the Life and Growth of the Madison Church of Christ" (Pasadena, CA: Fuller Theological Seminary dissertation, 1986), 30.

10. Ibid., 69.

11. Ibid., 97, 109, 122.

12. Rebecca Manly Pippert, *Out of the Saltshaker & into the World: Evangelism as a Way of Life* (Downers Grove, Ill.: InterVarsity Press, 1979).

13. Linthicum, 148.

14. Ibid., 156, 160.

15. Billie Silvey, ed., *Trusting Women*, 23.

Chapter Six

1. Much of this chapter is adapted from a paper written for Eddie Gibbs' class in Effective Evangelism at Fuller Seminary.

2. Robert Kolb, *Speaking the Gospel Today* (St. Louis: Corcordia, 1984), 13.

3. George Barna, *Evangelism That Works* (Ventura, CA: Regal Books, 1995), 64.

4. Eddie Gibbs, "Church Growth through Effective Evangelism," Syllabus and Lecture Outlines, Pasadena, CA: Fuller Theological Seminary, 1998, "The Evangelizing Church," 2.2.

5. Charles Van Engen, "Constructing a theology of mission for the city," *God So Loved the City,* 249.

6. Ibid., 248-51.

7. Adapted from Billie Silvey, "Helping Urban Churches Grow," *Christian Chronicle* (October, 1995) 15.

8. Silvey, "Urban Churches Beckon," *Image Magazine* (July/August, 1996), 23.

9. Henri J. M. Nouwen, *In the Name of Jesus: Reflections on Christian Leadership* (New York, NY: Crossroad, 1994), 30.

10. Pippert, *Out of the Saltshaker*, 73.

11. Ibid., 110.

Chapter Seven

1. Philip Yancey, *The Jesus I Never Knew* (Grand Rapids, MI: Zondervan, 1995), 228.

2. Yancey, *Disappointment with God: Three Questions No One Asks Aloud* (New York: HarperPaperbacks, 1988), 155.

3. Ibid., 157.

4. Ibid., 159.

5. Ibid., 160.

6. Leighton Ford, *The Power of Story: Rediscovering the Oldest, Most Natural Way to Reach People for Christ* (Colorado Springs, CO: NavPress, 1994), 123.

7. Lewis A. Drummond, *The Word of the Cross: A Contemporary Theology of Evangelism* (Nashville, TN., Broadman, 1992), 294.

8. Yancey, *The Jesus I Never Knew,* 232.

9. Ibid., 233.

10. Ibid., 234.

11. Bernard L. Ramm, *His Way Out: A Fresh Look at Exodus* (Glendale, CA: Regal Books, 1974), 9.

12. Herbert Schlossbert, Samuel Vinay and Ronald J. Sider, eds., *Christianity and Economics in the Post-Cold War Era: The Oxford Declaration and Beyond* (Grand Rapids, MI: Eerdman's, 1994), 19.

13. Sider, *Rich Christians*, 89.

14. *Growing Together: Linking Regional and Community Development in a Changing Economy* (International Public Affairs Center, Occidental College, 1997), 5.

15. "Organizing and Operating a Life Skills Lab" (Memphis, TN: Memphis Area Community Services, unpublished, 1992), 1.

16. Names of students have been changed to protect their privacy, but the situations are actual.

17. Much of what follows is based on Billie Silvey, "It's Not What You'd Expect," a symposium on Poverty and Possessions sponsored by *Leaven* at the 1998 Pepperdine Lectures, printed in 6:3.

18. J. I. Packer, *Knowing God* (Downers Grove, IL: InterVarsity Press, 1973), 63.

19. Packer, 63-64.

Chapter Eight

1. Packer, *Knowing God*, 230-231.

2. Ibid., 231-2.

3. Kolb, *Speaking the Gospel*, 187.

4. GTSC Consulting, "Culver Palms Life Skills Lab Project," Malibu, CA: Pepperdine University, December 2, 1997.

5. "Survey of Employment/Self-sufficiency and Related Course Interest among Parents at El Rincon and Linwood Howe Elementary Schools" Culver City, CA, February 1998.

6. Prayers quoted in this chapter are copied from my journals from the time.

7. Henry T. Blackaby and Claude V. King, *Experiencing God: Knowing and Doing the Will of God* (Nashville, TN: LifeWay, 1990), 119.

8. Lewis D. Solomon, *Microenterprise: Human Reconstruction in America's Inner Cities* (Cambridge, MA: Harvard Journal of Law and Public Policy, 1992).

Chapter Ten

1. Irving R. Warner, *The Art of Fund Raising* (Lincoln, NE: Authors Guild Backinprint.com, 2001), 21.

2. Sider, *Rich Christians*, 80.

3. Billie Silvey, "Reflections on Learning Grantwriting," Pasadena, CA: a directed study paper in urban mission submitted to Jude Tiersma Watson at Fuller Seminary, Fall 1999.

4. Since I wrote this, the federal government has offered a limited number of grants to religious organizations under its Faith-Based and Community Initiatives. The only grant I was able to apply for funded only 50 organizations, or one per state.

5. Mim Carlson, *Winning Grants Step by Step: Support Centers of America's Complete Workbook for Planning, Developing, Writing Successful Proposals* (San Francisco: Jossey-Bass, 1995).

6. Norton J. Kiritz, "Proposal Checklist and Evaluation Form" (Los Angeles: The

Grantsmanship Center, 1979).

7. Carla Rivera, *Los Angeles Times*, May 31, 1999, 1.

Chapter Eleven

1. Rosenblatt, *Wrestling with Angels*, 315.
2. Ibid., 333.
3. Ibid., 330.
4 Ibid., 331.
5. Ibid., 345.
6. Ibid., 337.
7. Drummond, *The Word of the Cross*, 312-313.
8. Ibid., 347.

Chapter Twelve

1. Bakke, *Urban Christian*, 71-72.

Chapter Thirteen

1. Kolb, *Speaking the Gospel*, 194-6, adapted.

Chapter Fourteen

1. Harold Shank, *Loosening Your Grip: Letting Go and Living in True Security* (Fort Worth, TX: Sweet Publishing Co., 1995), 8-9.

2. Ibid., 29.

Annotated Bibliography

Allen, C. Leonard. *Distant Voices: Discovering a Forgotten Past for a Changing Church*. Abilene, TX: ACU Press, 1993. An account of historical movements and individuals whose distinctive approaches helped advance various areas of emphasis among Churches of Christ. See particularly Chapter 13, "God's Chosen Vessels" for David Lipscomb's view of and ministry to the poor.

Bakke, Ray, with Jim Hart. *Urban Christian: Effective Ministry in Today's Urban World*. Downers Grove, IL: InterVarsity Press, 1987. An evangelist, Ray Bakke shares the fruit of over twenty years living and working in Chicago, while considering local ministry from an international context. He combines a pastor's heart and a scholar's mind.

Drummond, Lewis A. *The Word of the Cross: A Contemporary Theology of Evangelism*. Nashville, TN: Broadman Press, 1992. Drummond moves easily from the theoretical to the practical in this rich study of the basis and spread of the gospel, and the Christian's response to God's work in the world. A balanced study of evangelism, worship and service.

Kolb, Robert. *Speaking the Gospel Today: A Theology of Evangelism*. St. Louis, MO: Concordia Publishing House, 1984. Moving from the theological basis to teaching and living the gospel of Jesus in a world that needs good news.

Linthicum, Robert C. *City of God, City of Satan: A Biblical Theology of the Urban Church*. Grand Rapids, MI: Zondervan Publishing House, 1991. A good discussion of living and serving as a Christian in an urban setting. Takes the concept of spiritual warfare a little too literally for my taste.

Rosenblatt, Naomi H. and Joshua Horwitz. *Wrestling with Angels: What Genesis Teaches Us About Our Spiritual Identity, Sexuality, and Personal Relationships*. New York, NY: Delta Trade Paperbacks, 1995. A Jewish woman looks at the heroes of the faith in relationship to their call, their personal relationships, and their place in their world. Great applications of historical situations to the challenge of living for God today.

Shank, Harold, Anthony Wood and Ron Bergeron. *Up Close and Personal: Embracing the Poor*. Joplin, MO: College Press, 2000. A very personal word from the trenches of urban ministry on how to serve the needy, based on insights derived from relationships with the people themselves.

Sider, Ronald J. *Rich Christians in an Age of Hunger: Moving from Affluence to Generosity*. Dallas, TX: Word, 1997. A revised edition of the definitive study of poverty, wealth, and Christian responsibility. See especially Chapter 5, "Thinking Biblically about Property and Possessions."

Van Engen, Charles and Jude Tiersma, eds. *God So Loves the City: Seeking a Theology for Urban Mission*. Monrovia, CA: MARC, 1994. A collection of essays combining biblical theology and practical urban ministry by an international team of experienced urban practitioners. Edited with valuable contributions by urban ministers and scholars at Fuller Theological Seminary. Combines stories, reflections and methodology.